M000086089

Praise for
The Elderwise Way: A Different Approach to Life with Dementia

The Elderwise Way affirms what those of us who have walked this path with a family member or friend knows: Every person's essence is immutable, regardless of the physical or cognitive changes they have endured. I read this book with joy.

— Ann Hedreen, Author, *Her Beautiful Brain*,
and Documentary Filmmaker

Reading about dementia can be hard and frightening. It is easy to become overwhelmed and discouraged. One of the core takeaways from many books is the belief that when someone is diagnosed with dementia, they are no longer there, lost to those who know and love them, no longer accessible or knowable. One reads and grieves.

However, reading *The Elderwise Way* has a very different effect. Based on a program now more than two decades old, the book summarizes the principles and practices of a unique program that is at the forefront of revolutionizing our understanding of how to be with people with cognitive loss.

This important book is filled with compassion, connection, humor and honesty. It reminds us of our own humanity and deep capacity for love. It is a book worth reading and rereading.

— Rebecca J. Crichton, Executive Director,
Northwest Center for Creative Aging

The Elderwise Way, written by a pioneer in work with those with dementia, is a short, deceptively simple book with profound insights. Sabersky provides guidance, support and communication tools to enhance the lives of those with memory loss. Care partners and professionals in the field will benefit from her sage advice. This is a welcome addition to the resources available to those doing this important work.

— Carin Mack, MSW, Memory Loss Programs Director,
Greenwood Senior Center, Seattle

From the day she first invited elders to share a meal, art and conversation around her kitchen table, Sandy Sabersky's commitment to the essential wholeness of all persons, regardless of cognitive ability, has impacted countless lives. Now, she offers another gift. In these pages, she invites us to a seat at the Elderwise table, generously sharing the practices and principles that underpin her remarkable adult day program and allowing us to follow in her pioneering footsteps. With its thoughtful blend of stories, reflections and practices, *The Elderwise Way* offers valuable insights for family caregivers and professionals alike.

— Marigrace Becker, Program Manager, Community
Education and Impact, University of Washington
Medicine, Memory and Brain Wellness Center

Compassion is at the heart of all the world's major belief systems: Buddhism, Islam, Judaism, Christianity. Compassion is also the heart and core of this brilliant new book. You need not be a location-based entity to honor people *The Elderwise Way*. Nor is this message only for those in relationship with elders. Read this book and learn the how and why of better treatment of people of all ages and cognitive states.

— Jeannette Franks, PhD, Gerontologist and author

This small book is a jewel. Always recognizing that "the person with dementia has not lost any spiritual ground," it reveals the deep respect *The Elderwise Way* shows for people with dementia.

The caregivers take time to create a beautiful, welcoming space in which the participants feel at home. The artistic component of the Elderwise program nourishes the soul of all present in the day, participants and caregivers alike. The beautiful poems by David Leek are a wonderful enrichment to the book's content.

It was such a pleasure and honor to read *The Elderwise Way*. It is my hope that it finds its way to many caregivers.

— Nettie Fabrie, author and former Director of Pedagogy,
Seattle Waldorf School

Learning about dementia in the ivory tower is one thing, but unless we understand what is really happening in the field, we cannot hope to help our patients, family members and professional caregivers. *The Elderwise Way* explains basic principles that can be used by anyone to enrich the existence of those whose lives are impacted by dementia. Even though such individuals may no longer be able to memorize or recall information, they still feel emotion and can grow spiritually. One of the most salient points that Sabersky makes is that the decrease in cognitive functionality does not prevent spiritual growth.

The principles embodied by Elderwise are applicable to any individuals who might have the opportunity to interact with frail elders. If I am lucky, I would like someday to join Elderwise as a participant. *The Elderwise Way*— what a concept!

— Masa Sasagawa, ND, PhD, Director of Research
Laboratories, Assistant Research Scientist/ Adjunct Faculty,
Bastyr University

THE ELDERWISE WAY

A Different Approach to Life with Dementia

SANDY SABERSKY

AND

RUTH NEUWALD FALCON

ABOUT THE AUTHORS

Sandy Sabersky has, for all of her adult life, focused her professional and personal attention on the fields of aging and spiritual growth. These two threads were brought together when she co-founded Elderwise, an adult day enrichment program with a spirit-centered approach to working with people with dementia, in 1997, after more than two decades as a Physical Therapist. She is grateful for all the opportunities Elderwise has given her: for learning, growth and expansion. She appreciates the opportunities it brings to express herself—artistically, verbally and through movement—and for the community of fellow travelers.

Ruth Neuwald Falcon is an Emmy Award-winning editor, writer, producer, web content creator and blogger. She has also run a small business and been executive director of two non-profit organizations. Combining the creativity and aesthetics of a director with the technical knowledge of the editor, Ruth relishes the joys and satisfactions of working collaboratively with other authors and filmmakers. www.RuthNeuwaldFalcon.com

© 2020 Sandy Sabersky

Print ISBN 978-1-09830-885-8

eBook ISBN 978-1-09830-886-5

Some names and identifying details in this book have been changed to protect the privacy of individuals.

All rights reserved. This book, or parts thereof, may not be reproduced in any form without permission.

For permission requests, contact info@elderwise.org

Excerpt from KITCHEN TABLE WISDOM by Rachel Naomi Remen, M.D., copyright © 1996 by Rachel Naomi Remen, M.D.. Used by permission of Riverhead, an imprint of Penguin Publishing Group, a division of Penguin Random House LLC. All rights reserved.

Poetry by David Leek used by permission.

First printing, 2020.

Designed by BookBaby

Photos by Olivia Lohmann and Annie Koziol

Cover art by Rick King

Paintings by Elderwise participants

Published by Elderwise®

Spirit-Centered Care™

531 NE 112th Street

Seattle, WA 98125

www.elderwise.org

Printed in the United States of America.

To my dear family and friends who travel closely with
me through this journey of life.
Sandy Sabersky

To my friends, for their steadfast gifts of loyalty,
acceptance and, most of all, love.
Ruth Neuwald Falcon

TABLE OF CONTENTS

Acknowledgments 1

Ode to the Table 5

Foreword 7

Preface 11

Introduction 13

Chapter 1:   The Program Is 19

    The program is the intangibles 20

    The program is slowing down time: The Elderwise Time Zone 20

    The program is the environment 21

    The program is the rhythm 23

    The program is the practice 25

    The program is being present in the moment 26

Chapter 2:   Supporting The Frail Elder *The Elderwise Way* 29

    Who is the frail elder? 31

The Feast of Life 34

Chapter 3:   The Elderwise Day 35

    The day begins 36

    Entering the day 37

    "Supported Coffee Shop" 40

    Creating individually and together 42

    Painting 44

    Working with clay 48

    Collage 50

    Time to kick back 50

    Movement 52

    Lunch 54

After-lunch discussion 56

The day concludes 59

Chapter 4:   The Concept of Wholeness 61

What makes us whole? 61

Mind does not equal brain 64

Chapter 5:   The Foundation of Spirit-Centered Care 67

Recognizing one's own essence 68

Recognizing the essence of others 69

The experience of equality 70

Awareness of the us-versus-them phenomenon 71

Deep listening 72

Chapter 6:   The Practice of Spirit-Centered Care 75

Spiritual health 76

Older models of caring for those with dementia 79

Spirit-Centered Care 80

It's All Good 83

Chapter 7:   Aging and the Senses 85

Our changing relationship with the senses 85

The concept of the twelve senses 87

Transforming our relationship with the senses 88

The God of Small Things 89

Chapter 8:   The Four Physical Senses 91

Touch 91

Sense of life 94

Movement and Balance 96

A Confusion of Directions 100

Chapter 9:   The Four Feeling or Emotional Senses 101

Smell 102

Taste...103

Vision 104

Temperature 105

Listening...108

Chapter 10: The Four Spiritual Senses..111

Hearing 112

Speech 113

Thought...114

Ego...118

Tools for transforming our lives...119

Chapter 11: Dementia and Spirituality..121

The growing sense of heart...123

Our final new experience 127

Chapter 12: Caregiving...129

The Dementia Care Partner 129

Giving care as a spiritual practice 130

Learning to quiet one's self..131

Chapter 13: Continuum of Care 137

Physically smaller, but not spiritually smaller 139

Not Wrong, Not Right...141

In Conclusion 143

Appendix 1:

The Seeds for Elderwise..147

A profession, but not a calling 150

Making my vision a reality..152

Appendix 2: Reflections on facilitating art *The Elderwise Way* 155

Bibliography...159

ACKNOWLEDGMENTS

Swami Bhaskarananda showed me how to walk the walk of an ethical and conscious life.

My husband—also known as The Founding Spouse—David Merz, never said no. He didn't say no when I wanted to invite people with memory loss into our home. He didn't say no when I asked him to put rails in the living room for exercise. He didn't say no when I asked him to design and build art carts for us to use in our outreach program. He helped me schlep, listened to all my stories, supported me in all my struggles, and is always there for me in ways large and small.

My parents, Bettina and Rolf Sabersky, despite their struggles as immigrants who fled Europe for their lives, continued to grow and learn and love, always giving me the support to grow in my own way.

My children, Erika, Claire and Martin, grew up from an early age with a houseful of frail elders, both appreciating and tolerating the incursion into their home. They listened to me and supported me along the way, always rooting for me and Elderwise.

When I look at photographs from the early days of Elderwise, we all look so young! We've gotten older together. Some of us have died, some have moved on to other careers. It gives me particular delight and satisfaction when Elderwise is a stepping stone for young people to begin their careers in social work, nursing, counseling, or occupational therapy.

I am grateful to Cally Fulton for taking the leap of founding Elderwise with me. She helped me set the tone of community and relationship on which Elderwise is built.

Elderwise and I were fortunate that Fran Dunlap joined the team very early on. She was the embodiment of our philosophy, enthusiastic beyond measure, open-heartedly sharing her myriad interests and gifts with us. Her contributions of music and art, light and joy, infused Elderwise with a spark that is still there today.

Annie Koziol has been the Elderwise Operations Director since its early years. She's got my back and capably does everything from grants to book-keeping to making sure we have enough supplies—whatever is needed to make Elderwise thrive. I am so grateful for her caring, commitment and hard work, and rely on her straightforward and honest assessment of any situation. An avid gardener, she brings flowers every week that become part of the Elderwise centerpiece!

Diana Cheairs's quiet presence was soothing to us all. Artistic, holistic, broadminded, she had two official roles with Elderwise: facilitator and cook. And even after she stopped working with Elderwise on a regular basis, we knew we could call on her when an additional facilitator was needed. Her daughter, Cayce Cheairs, worked with us as first a facilitator and then later as a program coordinator. She continues to carry *The Elderwise Way* into her professional life.

Alline Thurlow intuitively understood Elderwise as soon as she walked in the door. Over the years, she offered her humor, her creativity, her ideas, and her friendship to me and to Elderwise. She was the first person who helped me envision this book, as she started to put the various pieces into some order.

Maria Lucas was the cook for many years. She brought wonderful organic foods and recipes, and was very much a part of the life of the program.

Tamara Keefe is an amazing artist who brings great integrity to whatever she does. As Outreach Coordinator, she developed many relationships with the larger community and started a number of programs that are still going.

Mari Nakamura shared her kind and gentle spirit with Elderwise as a volunteer. She enjoyed being with the older participants, especially since her own mother was far away in Japan, and appreciated being able to practice English, while serving in any way she could.

Bonnie Bledsoe brings light and delight to us all with her warmth, understanding and humor. She is a wonderful artist who continues to coax out the artist out in all of us.

Mollia Jensen brought her remarkable skill at understanding nuance to her position as Program Director. Something of an alchemist, she kept an eye on various simmering pots, knowing when to add the right ingredient to the right pot, and when to just let things cook quietly. I am grateful for her dedication and conscientious devotion to Elderwise.

Jeannette Ruby, a former Executive Director, is a doctor who had a lot of faith in Elderwise. She appreciated the philosophy and worked hard to carry it forward. She is the first person to put this book into manuscript form, an important step along the way.

Heather Timken and Elisabeth Mitchell are the original members of a committee whose goal was to guide this book through to publication. They are both amazing people with whom it is a pleasure to work.

Rebecca Crichton is a longtime Elderwise board member who has become a dear friend. She's kind, compassionate, understanding, and a master of bringing the right people together. It is her skills as a connector that brought me and Ruth Neuwald Falcon together.

Ruth Neuwald Falcon is the reason this book is in your hands. We worked on it together, page by page, word by word. She helped keep me grounded, as we found language to best convey what I felt was most important about Elderwise and my journey. It was a privilege to go through this experience with her. The longer we worked together, the better our process became and the more we appreciated each other. We also had a good time, which is, as you will see, one of the goals of *The Elderwise Way*.

There are too many more people—from staff to board members to volunteers—to mention by name. They have all generously given of their hearts and creativity along the way. I have appreciation for each and every one of them.

Elderwise doesn't exist in a vacuum. We are proud to be part of a large community of like-minded organizations and are especially grateful to those professionals who recognized early on that Elderwise was worth paying attention to. Here I would like to mention Carin Mack, a passionate advocate for seniors and those with dementia in particular, who was the first to recognize that this was an approach worth encouraging.

Because our groups are small, we truly get to know these wonderfully interesting elders. Looking back over the years, I can still see many of them in my mind's eye. We shared prayers and laughter, tears and ideas. They've opened my heart and deepened my appreciation for what is possible as we age in general, and as we age with dementia in particular. It has been a joy and privilege to be with them.

ODE TO THE TABLE

by *Bettina Sabersky*

Oh humble table it's to you
We sing a song of praise
With paint and flowers, brush and clay
You set our souls ablaze.

Oh faithful table, you are there
in summer, spring and fall
You're decked with beauty, food and art
To nourish one and all.

Oh sturdy table we all long
to share your loving space.
It's by your side we find real joy
and friends we can embrace.

FOREWORD

A meeting of the minds: Finding community at Elderwise

When considering the constantly changing face of family, what it means, and what it involves, I feel that whenever and wherever *anyone* can find a sense of belonging, it is a gift. This applies even more so to our young ones and our elders who, for too many obvious reasons, are at risk of becoming isolated or neglected.

What does this sense of belonging offer, and why do I consider it a gift? For me, beyond its soft and comfortable feelings, belonging brings responsibility and accountability; values and actions that are inherent to both giving and receiving. To give and to receive spring from the fullness of belonging here, of being here in relationship with others, and the felt sense of acceptance for who you are—your essence.

At Elderwise, *here* is not just a location. *Here* is alive with intention and the potential of now. When you enter the main room of Elderwise, you will see a large, oblong table with soft, wooden, curved edges surrounding a light-grey matte Formica finish. At least ten comfortable chairs (with extra cushions as needed) can be seen close by.

I bet if you were to look with a very "fine-toothed" eye at the table's surface, you would be able to discern—despite the table's multiple daily cleanings throughout its long lifetime—a quiet palette of embedded color, and maybe even some crumbs hiding in the seams where the Formica meets the wood. To me, these subtle findings remain as a silent, but powerful, testament to the truth embodied by this table: Each and every person who sits at the table is given the opportunity to experience a sense of belonging.

As an Elderwise staff member, every time I sat down at the table to facilitate an activity with the participants, or to engage in problem-solving or future-weaving with other facilitators, I, too, felt that sense of belonging. But, for me, belonging was epitomized by the palpable sense of acceptance I witnessed in others. It was clearly apparent as each participant's unique perspective on a given concept or topic was invited and welcomed. And, in the comfortable silence that settled over the room when everyone was focused on their painting, that sense of belonging was most obvious to me. It was as though the silent stillness embraced each and all, allowing the sense of isolation or separation to lift away. Finding acceptance within a group of people that are not your family, but rather a group of your peers—your equals, no matter what your age, stage of life, or state of mind—is empowering. And empowerment provides space and support to venture out and explore new territory.

Whether you are personally experiencing dementia, witnessing it in a friend or loved one, attempting to create a positive artistic or movement experience for those with dementia, listening to the thoughts of others, or sharing insights or concerns, dementia is new territory. The Elderwise program approaches this territory with open eyes, an open heart, and an open mind. A willingness to see, feel, and think outside the usual box is an unwritten prerequisite for those taking a seat at the table. This applies to all who join Elderwise, whether participants, staff, or board members. All share the attitude of meeting and honoring both the gifts and the limitations that we each carry with us, while looking a bit deeper to discover what we may create together. This attitude imbues the programming, planning, and policies that support every aspect of Elderwise.

Watching participants sincerely welcome each other, or someone new to *their* community around the Elderwise table, was a valuable experience for me. I recall recognizing that we must be doing some very special work, when I witnessed the entire demeanor of one usually somber participant change before my eyes: As she accepted the warm hand of a friend into hers and began sharing something she'd seen on the bus ride to Elderwise that morning, her face lit up. Another poignant moment occurred when another participant, broom in hand and grateful to be helping by sweeping the courtyard, looked up and sincerely asked if she couldn't just live here with us. I found myself wishing that she could.

But, it's not all sweetness and easygoing around the Elderwise table all the time: Dementia offers the chance to dance with the darker side, too. These occasions call upon the strengths and skills of facilitators and participants alike. When, for example, an inappropriate and awkward remark was made during an activity, it was as though the community around the table deflected the remark; someone offering a response that honored the person, while another shifted the group's attention, demonstrating the difference each individual can make to a group dynamic.

I am personally richer for the friendships and wisdom I gained through my work with Elderwise. The friendship of both staff members and participants, the new skills, and the deep understanding that I've been lucky enough to carry forward after leaving that community are the legacies of Elderwise that I gratefully look to and use in many arenas of my life and work.

Alline Thurlow, former Elderwise facilitator
July 2019

PREFACE

I work with people with dementia. You may think that this must be really difficult, but it's not. One of our Elderwise participants, let's call her Marta (throughout the book, names have been changed to protect people's privacy), once told me, "When I tell people that I have Alzheimer's disease, their mouths drop, and they say, I'm so sorry! But I look at them and say, Look at me! I'm still here, and I can still *do things*." I would also add that Marta can still feel things and see things and experience things.

Compassion resides within the essence of each one of us and reveals itself when gently touched by its reflection. One who is not familiar with being around elders, and especially elders with dementia, might find themselves quite surprised to find the mood around the table at Elderwise—the adult day program started at my kitchen table more than two decades ago—to be joyful, thoughtful, full of gratitude and mutual support. In this atmosphere of humor and friendship, I have been witness to the almost daily demonstration of compassion that this kind of environment fosters—it is the juice of life that's an elixir for all ages.

Over the past 20-plus years, I have spent many of my days sitting around this table with different groups of people, most of whom have some degree of dementia. The fact is, there are few people with whom I'd rather be sitting around a table. It is for them that I am writing this book.

I am writing this book because the treatment of older people matters deeply to me, especially those older individuals whom I refer to as *frail elders*—those who are isolated and/or limited due to physical, cognitive, or emotional changes. It is my deep desire that those who manage the living environments of the frail elder will, through this book, come to a richer understanding of their role. Through offering deep respect and appreciation to the hands-on caregivers who serve their populations, directors and managers can create an attitude of equality in the workplace, and this attitude will be carried forward into every relationship that exists within the organization or facility.

And I am writing this book because I recognize the value to society as a whole if frail, at-risk elders are treated well. Older people are in danger of becoming isolated, closed, and hardened in their habits if they withdraw from the world as their mobility or clarity of thinking decreases. This risk is further compounded when older people vent their frustration with their own waning abilities upon those they are closest to. But if we can create an environment that supports frail elders in becoming more adventurous, more joyful, more tolerant, and more trusting, we then give them opportunities to continue their growth and to move toward their death with more openness.

When we as direct caregivers tap into creativity, deep joy, and understanding, we raise the quality of life for elders, thereby making a better society for us all. A society that values, nurtures, and supports the growth of elders cannot help but model this respect for others throughout all stages of the lifespan.

Lastly, I am writing this book because I have been gifted with growing personally through working with a population most people want to avoid, and I wish to share that opportunity with others. What if, instead of dreading being with old people, we could enjoy our time with them? What if, by bringing out the light in their eyes, we discover that time with them brings increased light and joy to our own lives?

I invite you to enter this book and make these discoveries for yourself.

Sandy Sabersky
Seattle, Washington, January 2020

INTRODUCTION

The original Elderwise group arrives at my house.

Elderwise—a unique approach to aging through cultural enrichment and deep respect for all people—started in my kitchen in 1997. In the more than two decades since, its values of respect and dignity have infused the Seattle community. Elderwise acts as an agent of change in our society, doing so through our model adult day center, our teaching and outreach programs, and our leadership in the field of enriched care for elders.

Perhaps if you are reading this book you have a spouse or parent or friend, a brother or sister, aunt or uncle, who is a frail elder. Or maybe you yourself are cognitively challenged with dementia, physically challenged by arthritis, or emotionally challenged with depression. Perhaps you are a family caregiver in your home, or a professional caregiver, or part of the management staff in a private home, an adult family home, or a supported living facility. Or you might be an activities director, nurse, social worker, or therapist. One way or another, it is likely you have direct involvement with a frail elder through family or work, or indirect involvement through care-facility management. Whatever your connection, we all share a common interest in the well-being of frail elders.

In this book, I explain both the tangibles and the intangibles of the Elderwise program—from the philosophical to the practical—and trust that you will find concepts that resonate with you. Together, we can bring a deep sense of respect and dignity into all that impacts and embraces advanced aging in our society, doing so through our attitudes and ways of being in the world.

In Chapter One, *The Program Is*, we explore some of the philosophical underpinnings that provide the unseen reasons for the program's success. The intangibles—the environment, the rhythm, the practice, being present—all of these things make up *The Elderwise Way*.

I refer to the *frail elder* throughout this book when, in reality, many of our Elderwise participants are neither old nor, apparently, frail. And, like many descriptive labels, it is one that may bring to mind different images and ideas for each of us.

In Chapter Two, *Supporting the Frail Elder the Elderwise Way*, with the awareness that frail elder is not a perfect term, I offer what I mean when I use it and discuss how we at Elderwise design our program to support the needs of each individual—frail or not—while continuing to honor their essential wholeness.

Chapter Three takes us through a day at Elderwise—what we do and the spirit in which we do it. There is a natural flow that we cultivate, one of ritual and repetition, which leads us seamlessly through the day. For people with memory loss, transitioning from one activity to the next can be jarring. Because of the flow of *The Elderwise Day*, these transitions happen naturally and organically, eliminating the struggles that can come with shifting activities.

Chapter Four, *The Concept of Wholeness*, considers the question of what makes us whole and how exploring this question illuminates some of the unconscious assumptions we make about people as they face different kinds and degrees of debilitation.

In Chapter Five, *The Foundation of Spirit-Centered Care*, I introduce a defining Elderwise term. This core concept of Spirit-Centered Care is based on acknowledging that each person has a fundamental essence, one that is immutable. It exists regardless of physical or cognitive change. This essence is the most fundamental part of a human being. It is something that is untouched by whatever mental or physical debilitation occurs. Spirit-centered care is at the foundation of Elderwise and informs everything we do.

In Chapter Six, *The Practice of Spirit-Centered Care*, we move from the philosophical underpinnings of Spirit-Centered Care to its practical application in day-to-day circumstances and activities. In this chapter, we ground the ephemeral.

Chapter Seven, *Aging and the Senses*, considers the importance of stimulating our senses as we age in ways that can facilitate personal growth, even while dealing with mental and physical decline. This provides a frame for developing our programming, with the conscious goal of stimulating a variety of senses—even some we don't normally consider as such—during the course of a day. We go into detail about *The Four Physical Senses* in Chapter Eight; *The Four Feeling or Emotional Senses* in Chapter Nine; and *The Four Spiritual Senses* in Chapter Ten.

The conviction that personal growth is still possible even when one has lost cognitive powers is one of the essential components of *The Elderwise Way*. There are profound consequences to this approach, which I explore in Chapter Eleven, *Dementia and Spirituality*.

Caregiving is a tall order for those who take on that role, and my hat is permanently off to those who undertake it. In Chapter Twelve, I offer approaches and attitudes that may ease some moments and may deepen your relationships with those living with memory loss.

Chapter Thirteen, *Continuum of Care*, demonstrates that the philosophy of *The Elderwise Way* can be applied even to a person with seriously advancing disease. After a certain point, a person living with dementia may no longer be able to process and take in the whole group. The concept of continuum of care recognizes this and explores adjusting the supported opportunities to match the needs of the individual.

Interspersed, you will find poetry by David Leek, a thoughtful and intelligent man with Alzheimer's disease. A counselor by profession, a Buddhist in spiritual practice, he only started writing poetry after his Alzheimer's diagnosis. I heard David read his poems at a memory loss event and was deeply moved, so much so that I requested permission to include some of his work in this book. His poetry invites us to view the world through the eyes of someone living with dementia. And his words are beautiful.

The framework of the Elderwise day program has been fine-tuned over time and in several different locations, but I want to make clear that I am not presenting a recipe. Rather, I am offering a reframing of the principle of caring for others, incorporating into it the desire to create something beautifully deep and rich for yourself and those in your care. The specifics of this framework are for a four-hour structured program that flows seamlessly. Depending upon the needs of the population you are serving, you can adjust the length and choose which elements of the program you would like to include. Your heart, as well as your mind, will tell you how to best integrate these fundamentals into your days. You can begin with the specifics of how our day is structured, or you can dive into the conceptual underpinnings of the program.

As this book is entering the final stages prior to publication, we are three months into the Covid-19 pandemic and Elderwise itself is in the process of adapting the program to the strictures required by the need for social isolation. We are translating what we do into a surprising new medium, as we adapt video conferencing to the needs and requirements of the population we are continuing to serve. We have started to set up themed meetings that include sharing morning coffee, discussion, movement, storytelling, even art, and are very excited to see how well our activities and philosophy adapt to the new circumstances.

We are all seeing that physical proximity, while certainly preferable, is not necessarily required to profoundly connect with others. In fact, even when the time comes that we are allowed to meet again in person, we plan to continue with an online program for participants who otherwise wouldn't be able to access Elderwise, whether because of distance or other reasons. We also plan to continue to use video conferencing for family support groups, thus enabling caregivers to stay home and connected at the same time. In addition, we are developing online training for professional and lay caregivers that will allow us to expand the reach of the Elderwise approach.

It is our hope that, whatever the current personal and societal circumstances you find yourself in, the methods and attitudes that you will glean from reading this book will enrich your life and those with whom you are connected.

CHAPTER ONE:

The Program Is

Welcome to the warmth of Elderwise.

When Karen started looking for a daycare program for her mom, she approached it the way she approached her job in a large corporation: she developed a spreadsheet with columns for important tangible information—data such as caregiver-to-client ratio, cost per hour, hours of operation, number of activities, distance from home. She assigned a sliding point scale for each data set. Her plan was to select the program with the highest number of points.

But when she got in touch with Elderwise and our director explained that every day we made tea, exercised a bit, painted, and had a discussion over lunch, she, in her own words, "got stuck." *Make tea?* There was no column for tea making. She questioned further—*What about field trips?* No, we don't do field trips, our director told her. Despite being unable to imagine that spending four hours in this way would stimulate her mother, she was so desperate for help that she accepted our invitation to bring her mom for a trial visit. This is what she said some weeks after that visit:

"Walking into Elderwise was like entering a friend's living room—there was nothing institutional about the space. That was the first surprise. No fluorescent lighting! There were comfortable chairs, art on the walls, a vase filled with flowers in the middle of the table. Before I knew it, my mom—with a big smile on her face—was dancing with one of the participants during the exercise session. After exercise, we had lunch. The staff and the participants all sat around a large wooden table together. I still remember the discussion topic: *What traits were handed down to you from your mom or dad?* But what I remember most is that each person had the opportunity to talk and each person was listened to. My mom started the next week."

The program is the intangibles

This exacting daughter came to realize that the measure of the quality of the Elderwise program is in the *intangibles*. You can read the haiku that we write together, view the watercolor paintings, or share our discussion topics, and all of these things are important and enriching. But the answers to the deeper questions, the ones that Karen was seeking to find in her spreadsheet, lie between the lines: in the tranquility around the table; in the personal qualities the facilitators bring to the program; in the life they give to the activities; in the connections that grow among everyone each and every day.

The program is slowing down time: The Elderwise Time Zone

We all operate in this world at different speeds. Some of us are fast thinkers and talkers; others are slower. Some are quick to action; others want to ponder more. When we form friendships, we tend to choose those who are, so to speak, in our own orbit. I very much enjoy the company of those in a faster orbit than mine, but I find it exhausting if I spend too much time at that speed. This is part of the reason I like working with frail elders: We interact and function in a slower orbit.

As soon as you cross the threshold into the Elderwise space, you enter a different time zone.

I have come to refer to this concept as *slowing down time*. As soon as you cross the threshold into the Elderwise space, you enter a different time zone. This slower way of being is perfect for frail elders. It envelops the individual in much the same way that a warm or beautiful environment does. This unhurried pace allows the person with dementia, or any other loss, to relax, open up, and blossom.

The program is the environment

So this is one of the first things you notice when entering the Elderwise space: time has slowed down. You can breathe more deeply. Your body starts to relax. And, while we are more than our physical bodies and the Elderwise environment is more than the physical space, our goal is to create within the physical space the right environment for a frail elder to blossom, to unfold and open up. I like to imagine a petri dish, one of those small glass or plastic dishes used in a laboratory to grow bacteria. The task for the lab technician is to provide the optimum kind of medium, or nourishment, in order to create just the right environment for the bacteria to grow, thrive, and multiply.

In much the same way, we at Elderwise attend to the comfort and nourishment of each person. Our intention is that people will open, blossom, and feel well in our environment. It is an environment that supports individuals in body, mind, and spirit, and one that is conducive to deep, personal growth. As the mind seeks beauty, which feeds the soul and brings it warmth, we strive to create a beautiful environment.

We do this by paying attention to the temperature, the arrangement of furniture, how movement flows in natural patterns throughout the space, and also what can be seen, smelled, and heard within that space. All these factors and more are taken into consideration as we do our best to create an environment where people can relax the tight protective hold they have on themselves.

In many facilities serving elders, you'll see flyers, notices, and advertisements that take up many of the public walls. The rest are often covered with childish displays of seasonal motifs and holiday greetings. Paper plates, plastic spoons, metal folding chairs, and card tables are common items in these facilities. None of this is wrong in and of itself, but when taken as a whole, these practices contribute to the sense of a cold, sterile, and hard environment. It also infantilizes the elders, who may indeed have declining abilities, but are not, in fact, children.

An environment need not be fancy or elegant—both of which can be rather chilly—to be truly inviting. Old wooden chairs that are a bit worn, china dishes that may have a few chips, an old blue glass bottle used as a vase—these are objects that can make for an environment that is truly cozy and welcoming.

The aim is to have a conscious intention to create beauty. There can be touches of loveliness in the well placed vase; flowers, small objects, or stones displayed a certain way; a pretty cloth that covers the card table. Any object handmade with care can be displayed intentionally: a thoughtfully hung painting, a wooden box, or a simple carved stick invites an easy focal point and draws our attention beyond ourselves.

The Elderwise Way is to create an environment that opens and expands all who enter.

With aging, and especially with physical or cognitive deficits, one risks the possibility of becoming more closed or hardened. *The Elderwise Way* is to create an environment that opens and expands all who enter, an environment that elicits delight in flowers or newly formed buds, an environment through which we merge with beauty. The Elderwise environment offers our participants the pleasure of seeing the paintings they created themselves hanging on the wall; it offers delight in the warmth, the caring, and in a feeling of comfort and security, knowing that, as much as possible, one's needs will be attended to.

This environment is one that visitors, family members, and even hired caregivers enjoy as well. They may be there to drop off a participant, but then realize they're not really in so much of a hurry after all, that they want to stay a little longer and share a cup of coffee. Our peaceful environment and slower speed are luxuries hard to find in today's fast-paced society.

Space is so important to Elderwise that we have made it our tagline— *Elderwise: Creating space to age well.* This not only refers to the actual physical space in which we come together, but also to making room in our hearts to be open, accepting, and tolerant of others. We view space, in all realms, as opportunity.

The program is the rhythm

The next step is to create a rhythm that accommodates the needs and tastes of many individuals while promoting ease and community. Rhythms repeat like breathing: in and out, in and out. There are rhythms that are wonderfully soothing, like riding a train. The more regular in pattern, the more peaceful the rhythms are. From our own breathing, we can know if we are internally agitated or at peace. But we also have other rhythms in our bodies. Some we can be consciously aware of, such as the rhythm of our heartbeat; others, like the rhythmic flow of our cerebrospinal fluid, do not come to the level of conscious awareness.

There are also rhythms in our daily lives. We have the rhythms of when we get up, go to work, eat, and go to sleep. During the year, we have the rhythm of the seasons, the holidays, the start of the school year, the end of vacation— beginnings and endings. At Elderwise, there are many repeated practices from the beginning to the end of the day's session—removing a coat, lighting the morning candle, passing the hand wipes, saying the blessing. As we repeat these activities every day, in the same order, they become rituals that create a regular rhythm, a rhythm that soothes our souls and carries us smoothly through the day.

If you were drawing the rhythm of the day on a piece of paper it would look like a wave, going up for increased outward activity and going down to represent increased inward activity. This kind of flow creates a wave that participants, who may have trouble making transitions, can ride as they allow themselves to be carried with ease from one activity to the next.

Each part of the day brings its own unique rhythms as well. This allows participants and facilitators alike to bring their fresh selves and fresh attention to each changing activity. In general, the morning is social and outgoing; artwork time is quiet and reflective; physical exercise both releases and feeds our energy; and there's not a lot of talk during lunch as everyone is focused on their meal while sharing the common activity.

In our discussion time, focused listening provides a rhythmic flow of receiving and sharing ideas and feelings with others. Participants dig deep inside themselves to find the words to express their ideas and opinions. They love this chance to think, speak, and listen deeply. And, at the end of the day, we show the now dry paintings. Everyone at the table looks forward to this sharing of our artwork as the closing activity of the day, and we all miss this rhythmic exchange on the rare occasions when we run out of time.

If you were drawing the rhythm of the day on a piece of paper it would look like a wave, going up for increased outward activity and going down to represent increased inward activity. This kind of flow creates a wave that participants who may have trouble making transitions can ride as they allow themselves to be carried with ease from one activity to the next.

The program is the practice

One of the biggest intangibles of *The Elderwise Way* is the practice. The practice is the attitude with which we do things, the awareness with which we perform simple everyday actions. The practice is the way we are with people, and the care with which we endeavor to see others in their wholeness.

Here is another way to look at the practice: *It matters how....* It matters how you place the plate on the table, how you pour the coffee, how you move, and how you speak. This does not mean, however, that you have to feel watched all the time or that you have to be careful about everything you might do wrong. On the contrary, the practice of *It matters how* promotes a good feeling, one that comes with an awareness of what one is doing.

> The practice of *It matters how*
> promotes a good feeling,
> one that comes with an awareness
> of what one is doing.

Being aware, being mindful, and being conscious of every action, feeling, and thought brings the intangible and tangible results of love and care into the environment. This way of being is, of course, an aim, a goal, something we strive for: It is a practice that benefits the growth of the program facilitators, as well as the participants. This is how we bring the Elderwise philosophy into life.

The program is being present in the moment

Each moment is so rich. Let's say that all any of us have is right now. Let's say we remember nothing of what we did before, or how we got here. We look around. There is the beauty of a flower. The angle of the light. The shadows on the wall. Colors, fragrances, the feeling of the air—warm or cold—on our skin.

> Each moment is so full—if we take the time to notice where we are, what we are surrounded by, who we are with. In this way, the richness of a single moment expands like the sun's rays.

Each moment is so full—if we take the time to notice where we are, what we are surrounded by, who we are with. In this way, the richness of a single moment expands like the sun's rays. We do our best to create beauty, but to live completely and openly in the moment, whatever the conditions, is to bring ourselves more fully to life. And it prepares us to meet the next moment, the next thing offered to us, to see whatever might be hidden in it.

I'd like to tell you a little bit about Teresa, as she so richly embodied what a life lived with a heightened sense of the moment can offer. Teresa worked for the local utility company and was one of the first women in the city to climb electrical poles. When she came to Elderwise, she had Alzheimer's disease, yet she was always so present and so sincere in all her thoughts. I would sometimes see her walking in the park with her sister, Teresa gesturing to all of nature with delight. When I greeted her, she was again delighted, first to see me and then to share the experience of nature right in front of us. It's not that she knew exactly who I was. She would have been happy to see any friendly face and to share the beauty of nature with anyone who could meet her delight with their own. She exemplified the joy that can come with a heightened sense of the gifts of the moment.

As facilitators at Elderwise, we have to be aware of the flow of the day, be tuned in with one another and the participants, but we consciously strive to live in nothing but the present moment. We all do our best to live as fully in the moment as Teresa.

CHAPTER TWO:

Supporting The Frail Elder
The Elderwise Way

Have you ever wondered what it feels like to have Alzheimer's disease? I think it must be a little like walking on a busy, loud street on a chill and windy day. The cold picks up, and I hold my body a little more tensely; the wind picks up, and I pull my sweater tighter around myself. I want to cross the street but there are so many cars rushing by, and people all around me are talking—my stress levels are rising. Obstacles are everywhere.

Memory loss is, indeed, one of life's obstacles. A long time ago, I asked my mother what she believed about life. "It's one obstacle after another," she replied. "You just have to jump over them." She was jumping over obstacles until the end of her life. She wanted to maintain consciousness so that, even in those last days and hours, she wouldn't miss any opportunity to learn. "I'm happy to continue to live," she said, "as long as I learn something every day." Then she paused for a moment. "Or maybe every other day."

She wanted to be aware of her transition from this life. In front of her, I explained this to the hospice nurses who wanted to give her a little more morphine. "She's done everything she's needed to do," they said. "She's at peace with dying. Why not ease her process?" My job was to make them understand why we wanted to give her the minimum dose to keep her comfortable. When I finished, my mother nodded, pointed at me and said, "What she said."

We may have cancer; we may lose a job, or even a child; we all face our own mortality. The kinds of difficulties and losses we experience are endless in variety and severity. What do we seek in overcoming all these obstacles? We seek to learn and understand, and finally, we seek peace and joy, the *"my cup runneth over"* kind of joy, inward and peaceful. This process is not denied to people with memory loss. They can still learn and grow. With support, they can grow bigger hearts; they can be more accepting, more open and more peaceful. This helps people as they near the end of their lives and can possibly contribute to a more positive dying experience. As a society, we associate fear with the dying process. What I witnessed in my mother's dying was openness and curiosity, but no fear. Just as we protect ourselves on a cold day, people who do not get this support will frequently become more closed as they strive to protect themselves from the wind and the fast cars. They isolate, become paranoid and afraid, or they shut down as they watch endless hours of television.

Who is the frail elder?

At Elderwise, we think of a frail elder in the same way as any other elder except that their needs are greater and, therefore, they require additional support in one or more realms of body, mind, or spirit in order to function optimally.

We live in an independent age with a can-do spirit. This attitude can help us to accomplish many things. It does not, however, acknowledge our fundamental interdependency. We all need support to develop and mature as children and young adults. As we grow towards middle age, we need the support of our elders to guide the way and set an example of wisdom and acceptance. And whatever age we are, we all need environments in which we can function optimally. These ideal conditions are at least somewhat different for each of us.

Currently there are things I enjoy doing. In the physical realm, I enjoy walking, swimming, stretching, and breathing deeply. I like eating healthy food. In the realm of the mind, I enjoy creating; expressing through movement or song; intellectual engagement; and feeling a sense of community. And, on the spiritual level, I enjoy quiet, nature, prayer, ritual, and so on. I don't imagine that the general nature of the things I cherish will change with age and debility. Whether or not I can still do all the things that my body and mind allow me to do now, I will want all parts of me to be filled up and nourished on all levels. I might need someone to wheel me outside, so I can sit in nature, or take me to the beach, so I can put my feet in the water. As a frail elder, I will need the support of others to understand and help me satisfy my essential needs.

One of the goals of *The Elderwise Way* is to create circumstances in which anyone with whom we come in contact can be filled up and nourished on all levels. We are aware that we all need support in order to develop and thrive over the entire course of our lifetimes, and we also need certain environments in order to function optimally. When working with the frail elder, the goal is to create an environment and provide the appropriate support so that the person can flourish.

When the individual's deficit is in the *physical realm*, such as decreased movement, balance, circulation, vision, or hearing, the support needed is fairly straightforward, and that need is something we, as a society, are accustomed to addressing. Canes, walkers, wheelchairs, extra layers of clothing, eyeglasses, hearing aids, and a helping hand—all these adaptations help support the individual's physical needs and allow for their optimal ability to function in that realm.

The Elderwise Way is to provide supported opportunities for individuals so that they may meet their own needs for fullness and growth in the emotional, social, or intellectual spheres.

The frail elder may also need support in order to meet and satisfy *emotional, social, or intellectual needs*. These needs may be more difficult to discern and the required support may be somewhat less tangible. Not feeling well, lacking access to intellectual or social communication, being depressed, low in initiative, or having impaired thought processing can cause the individual to cross a functional line that also helps to define the frail elder.

The opportunity to express one's self and be listened to and understood on an appropriate level is important. The opportunity to listen to and learn from others; the opportunity to create thoughts, poetry, music, and art; and the opportunity to give and receive—all of these involve an exchange between the individual and the world. While not as tangible as the need for a cane or a hearing aid, the frail elder's most vital needs often include supported communication, supported creative opportunities, and supported socialization. How one might be supported in a spiritual way will be developed in Chapter Six, which is devoted to *Spirit-Centered Care.*

The Elderwise Way is to provide supported opportunities for individuals so that they may meet their own needs for fullness and growth in the emotional, social, or intellectual spheres, opportunities that allow each person to claim their full wholeness. The husband of one of our participants once said, "It's hard to describe how she is after attending Elderwise. The best way I can put it is that she seems kind of puffed up." I think this observation of his spouse being "puffed up" can be attributed to her being full and nourished in all facets of herself.

THE FEAST OF LIFE

by *David Leek*

Come to the table
Pull up a chair
The feast of life is here.

So many dishes to sample
Some hot, some cold,
Sour, sweet, and picanté too.

Don't be picky.
Try them all.
It's cheap to dither, to sniff and poke.
Sit down and begin.
Take a bite! Don't nibble!

Fill your mouth.
Enjoy the flavors and textures.
Don't rush!
Give each moment
The interest and curiosity it deserves.

Those moments never recur.
They rise and dispel
Like bubbles in champagne.
And yes, it will go flat some day.
But even that will be a lesson worth learning.

CHAPTER THREE:

The Elderwise Day

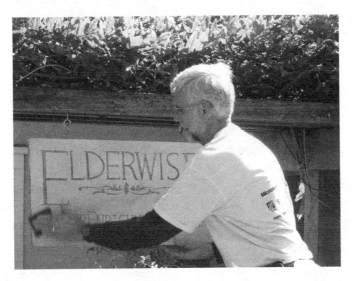

The Elderwise Way is to model an open heart and acceptance, kindness and humor, quiet and reflection, sharing and listening, respect and courtesy. Elderwise is a place for people to feel whole and quite all right just as they are. It is a place where various physical and cognitive impairments are a fact of life, not indicative of whom one is.

When Janice came to her trial day at Elderwise, the first thing she said as she was walking in was, "I'm not going to stay very long. I'll leave in a little while." Not only did she stay until the end of the group, engaged and smiling throughout, but the way she was talking to others was as if she were the old timer, rather than the new one to be welcomed. She was already so secure in this group that she could take on the role of being welcoming to others. In the space of one afternoon, *The Elderwise Way* had begun to work its magic.

The day begins

Giving thoughtful consideration to participant placement.

Our program formally starts at 10 a.m., but our inner and outer prepara-
tion for the participants starts before that. The facilitators get there early, not
only to set up the table and the art supplies but also to prepare themselves to
be fully present for each person and their needs, and each event as it arises.
We work on creating optimal seating arrangements. We often plan a general
focus for the day, and discuss how the art project and discussion topic can
expand on that concept. The other day, for example, our focus was peace
and we spent some time discussing how to structure our activities to explore
different aspects of peace, both inner and outer.

Entering the day

Sandy welcomes participants as they arrive.

How we greet participants is an important part of *The Elderwise Way*. We delight in welcoming each one into a space prepared just for them. We make an effort to greet each person as they step out of a bus, car or van, taking great care to make sure everyone is actively welcomed. This means taking time to look at the person, to take them in, and to determine how they are doing on this particular day. With a simple greeting and keen observation, the welcomer can discern quite a bit: *Is the participant well? Is she steady on her feet? Is he rested? Is she relaxed, or on edge? Is he happy to be here or preoccupied about something elsewhere?* Through initial, simple, caring attention, we can adjust our response accordingly. We may welcome with a hug or touch on the arm; we may put out a steadying hand, or respect the need for a little extra personal space. What we see in those brief greetings in the morning gives us an insight into how the day will go and allows us to calibrate to the needs of the group.

The other day, one woman came in looking a little off. Later in the day, she got a little irritable. Her caregiver had made a comment when they got there along the lines of, *We barely made it here today.* When I asked her what happened, all she said was her sister thought they were going to be late. Whatever set it off, she was more easily frustrated all day.

Another woman had just fallen—and taken her bus driver down with her as she tumbled. Her knee was skinned, her neck was bothering her, and we did our best to give her the attention she needed, both physically and emotionally. We fussed over her knee, let her family know what happened, checked in on the bus driver, and encouraged her to talk about the experience.

In a larger sense, *this* is their space. They cross a figurative as well as a literal threshold as they step into it, leaving the fast moving and often confusing world behind, to arrive in a place where things move a little more slowly. This is a place where people act and speak with care and warmth, a place in which a participant can expand and express the fullness of their being. Within this space, one can smell the coffee brewing, can listen and talk, freely and intimately, breathing in the goodness of the environment and breathing out a fuller expression of themselves. As Joyce often exclaims when she comes in, "I wish I could live here!"

Once the participant is inside, we take care to hang up hats, coats, and any additional layers required by Seattle's predictably variable weather, and, while paying great attention to each person's comfort and previously expressed preferences or desires, help them find their seat. We may drape a warm shawl over his shoulders, or give her a tissue if needed. The intent here is twofold: First, we are welcoming the participant from the outer world into the Elderwise space, a space where there is specific consideration given to each person's well being. Second, we take care of the small, outer physical needs so that everyone can relax and blossom fully.

From the entry area, we invite participants into the program room where nametags welcome them to their seat. In our early morning planning, we gave attention to physical placement and the attendant relationship development. There's one woman who enjoys being close to the man with the same name as her deceased husband, and this additional comfort level is a thing we take into consideration when planning seating. We think about who needs the support of a facilitator in close physical proximity and who needs to be sitting close to the bathroom.

Their physical needs are met so that attention and energy are available from within themselves, which enhances openness and willingness to meet the day.

Attention is paid to cleanliness, simplicity, and beauty. White china mugs anticipate something hot. Typically, we put fresh flowers or other objects from nature on the table. Beside them may be a candle in a ceramic candle holder made by a program participant. People often *ooh* and *ah* their wonder and delight in appreciation of the centerpiece. In retirement communities, where opportunities to leave the premises may be limited, it is especially important to bring a little of the outside inside. The window shades are adjusted so the sun shines nicely on our backs and not in our eyes. Shawls are given for the morning chill. All of this allows the participants to breathe in the comfort, relaxation, and security that radiates in the room. Their physical needs are met so that attention and energy are available from within themselves, which enhances openness and willingness to meet the day.

Slowly the spots at the table fill. People greet each other, adjusting their chairs just right, both in relation to the table and to one another. To be sure that everyone will be included, the program facilitators are mindful of whether all can hear and understand the gist of the conversation. The staff has taken great care in the placement of the nametags, being mindful of:

- physical needs (such as hearing or visual impairments);
- social needs (supporting the development of budding friendships, or their opposite—trying to limit potential competitiveness or other possible social irritants);
- and according to where staff support is otherwise needed at the table to enhance varied experience and interaction.

"Supported Coffee Shop"

We do our best to be attentive to how we serve.

This is what we call the first hour of the day. In Seattle, we have coffee shops on every block, sometimes even two or three. We meet our friends, socialize, gossip, solve the world's problems, and, of course, have coffee. When, because of impaired physical or cognitive abilities—or both—one can no longer initiate this type of social interaction, structured support can benefit a person's communal needs. One of the first things that people lose with memory loss is the ability to initiate activities. They might want to have coffee with their friends but are now unable to make such a meeting possible.

In the days when I did home care physical therapy, I would frequently stop at a coffee shop between house visits, and I saw, everywhere, whatever neighborhood I was in, local groups of friends who clearly met there on a regular basis. Coffee shops have become community meeting places, and when you lose the ability to either plan or get yourself somewhere on your own, you lose friendships. Not only can't I call and say, *Let's meet for coffee,* with memory loss, I don't even remember how to start a conversation. This is why we call it "supported coffee shop." Everything is provided: coffee, friends, and, when needed, subtle support for conversation. While we always come up with a topic in our morning planning, there are days when the talk just takes off on its own. But we've always got something in reserve to fall back on should the need present itself.

> The ideal of supported coffee shop is to create an environment for the natural socializing that occurs "out in the world" when getting together for coffee with friends.

After all the participants are comfortably settled, the two program facilitators assume their places at the table. One of the facilitators anchors the group. Ideally, this person projects calmness and radiates warmth and joy, embodying the magnet that draws the others in. It is the same as with children who so appreciate a lap: a safe and special place where no one is in a hurry, no one is running around with "a million things to do." We call this "holding the circle."

The other facilitator pours coffee or tea and serves toast. The smells are cheering. Each person has the opportunity to pass the toast plate, sweetener, and milk, as they pay attention to whether others have everything they need. The group as a whole is taking shape, a sense of community is forming. Welcomes are extended all around, and care is taken to consider each individual's preferences—coffee or tea; peanut butter, jam, or both, on their toast. Because we aim to create a coffee shop experience, we don't interfere with the group's social interaction unless it gets too quiet and participants seem to need support or an idea to talk about, or unless someone seems left out or unheard. This is a time for the participants to carry out their own social interactions, while we still tactfully protect those who are more socially vulnerable.

Sometimes conversation begins to flow while the staff is still in the background serving; at others, there is benefit to a staff member's interjection of some concept or question that may—or may not—be taken up by the group. For this aspect of the program, the facilitators usually have a couple of prompts in their literal or figurative back pockets: a photograph; some currently relevant quotes; ideas pertaining to nature; recent or upcoming holidays, trips, or visits; grandchildren; and so on. Often, the most alive conversations come out of something that has happened or some shared experience, like what it took to get there that day. These are often normal conversations you might hear anywhere: *The bus picked me up really early and it was a really long ride,* one might say. *My bus was late and I had to wait half an hour for it,* someone might reply. *I wasn't sure it was ever going to come!* We commiserate and we gently tease. The ideal of supported coffee shop is to create an environment for the natural socializing that occurs "out in the world" when getting together for coffee with friends.

Towards the end of the morning social hour, one begins to sense a readiness for change; murmurs start: *What are we going to paint today? Are we going to use clay?* It is time to gradually shift our energy from outward socializing to a more inward, creative time.

Creating individually and together

Reading a poem supports the transition from socializing to creating.

Someone once told me that all artistic work is therapeutic. We're not art therapists, but we do have a goal to help participants enjoy the creative and social aspects of making art together. It is a surprisingly social activity for it is about relationship—between the individual and the piece they are creating, and more subtly, between the artists in the room who are quietly painting or molding clay at the same time. And it is a way to express oneself other than verbally. For those who have trouble finding words, the creation of visual art offers another mode of expression for sensory impressions, memories, and emotions.

Making art together is a surprisingly social activity for it is about relationship—between the individual and the piece they are creating, and more subtly, between the artists in the room who are quietly painting or molding clay at the same time.

At Elderwise, our primary artistic media are wet-on-wet watercolors, working with clay to create forms that are later glazed, and sometimes, collage.

Painting

Deeply focused and engaged in his creative process.

Painting facilitates the outward creation of one's internal vision, feelings, or imagination. It contributes to satisfaction, self-esteem, and pride in one's artistic creation. The fluid motions of painting on wet paper promote a sense of freedom of movement, and make it possible to create a work of beauty, despite whatever physical limitations may be present. With age, arteries may be hardened and ways of being may become inelastic as well. The wet paint flowing over the wet paper and mixing with other colors to create new ones can help soften that stiffness.[1] This activity invites both inward and outward reflection, and works well as a creative experience within a community setting.

When painting on wet paper, the colors blend and beauty emerges. It's only our own restrictions that limit us. We've even had people who literally can hardly see: Janet is extremely vision impaired and her paintings are beautiful. Dan's vision was nearly gone, but he loved to paint. The vision inside his head was as clear and vivid as ever, and his mind was fully engaged in the ideas and in the feel of them coming out through his hand and his brush.

The inspiration and themes for the paintings are drawn from nature, the seasons, the feelings or moods of the day. Perhaps the full moon, the dreary

1   Norbert Glas, *The Fulfillment of Old Age* (Hudson: Anthroposophic Press, 1986), 66

rain, the first spring flowers, seasonal vegetables, or even a hot cup of coffee will spark creative inspiration. The facilitators may bring in components of a still-life arrangement or copies of photographs, or they may just capture the interest of the group by talking about the flow of a wave or the wind in a wheat field. Painting objects or scenes from nature can further help us become more aware of, and even in awe of, the world around us—the color of the sky, the details of the flower, the pattern and texture of a piece of cloth.

Wet-on-wet painting, as the term implies, involves attaching the paper to a painting board, wetting it and then sponging it off, so that the artist is left with a surface receptive to the fluidity of watercolors. Wet-on-wet watercolor painting with primary colors and quality materials invites a smooth and satisfying experience of color, color blending, shape, and beauty. We provide each participant with paints in small jars, each color having thicker paint at the bottom and more watery paint on the top of the jar, thus allowing for lighter and darker values. The artists' main tools are a one-inch watercolor brush and a rag. We may provide an additional, smaller brush for finer detail.

After everyone is gathered around the table and the wet painting boards are in front of the artists, we set the mood. A candle is lit in the center of the table. Often, one of the facilitators will read a poem or share a short comment—perhaps about the pink sky seen on a recent drive—and, with this, bring the painting idea to life.

Demonstrating how she is planning to start, the facilitator may suggest that the other artists start similarly. As the participants begin painting and become more and more absorbed in their own work, the facilitator continues working on her own painting and may interject only a time or two to share next steps. The participants may follow the instructor or their own inspiration. Often the room becomes very quiet while everyone is silently engaged with—or lost in—their own paintings. This kind of silence has a richness all its own and is the sign of a very successful painting program.

There are times when people's self-judgment gets in the way and they say, *"Oh no. I can't do this. I can't paint."* The first thing to do is empathize, not push into the resistance.

One of the greatest benefits to the individual participant is the therapeutic, meditative, and methodical rhythm of painting, and we encourage the independent experience of it as much as possible. The resulting piece of art will mean more to the artist if it is created without interference. The *process* of painting is fundamentally more important than the *outcome* of the artwork, yet, if someone is frustrated or asking for guidance, by all means, offer suggestions!

There are times when people's self-judgment gets in the way, and they say, *"Oh no. I can't do this. I can't paint."* The first thing to do is empathize, not push into the resistance. Then take the time to think about who this person is and how best to approach them. You might say, "I know you haven't done a lot of this before, but it's good to try new things as we age, to find different ways of communicating. We're not expecting a masterpiece. It's just about the process, to see if you can have a little bit of fun with it."

If they seem receptive, you might go on to say, "I'll give you an idea of how you might start. Take your brush and dip it in the water. Then dip it into some yellow paint and put some color on the page. Take a moment. Enjoy the color. Maybe you could take the sunlight, the yellow sunlight, and let it spread across the whole page, like opening the curtains on a sunny day. Then you might take some blue and put it on the yellow. And wow, a green meadow appears! So already you've got a sky and a meadow, and maybe that's enough. Or you might want to put some little green plants growing up from the bottom. Or you could add a tree, or some flowers."

By then, the person might have rediscovered their own tree in their own garden, or one remembered from long ago. This process can open memory and bring old images to life again.

Of course, there are people who continue to have a hard time. They're so bound by wanting what they paint to look like what they've been conditioned over a lifetime to think of as "good." One of the gifts of age—and it's one we encourage with our daily artwork—is permission to release some of those conditionings. It is such a pleasure to see people standing proudly beside their framed paintings at our annual auction, or holding a greeting card with an image of their work and their name on it.

If a participant still prefers not to paint, they can look at some art in a book. You can revisit the idea another day.

As we finish painting, the artists sign their work, some requiring assistance to do so. As we move the paintings to the drying rack, we pause to hold them up for the personal satisfaction of the artist and the admiration of the group. We hope that each person ends the session with a feeling of gratification in their own creation and that we, as a mutually supportive group sitting around the table, enjoy a deepened sense of community.

It is important to have a place to hang the paintings where others can view them. The artists, their families, and their caregivers, as well as the Elderwise staff, get tremendous enjoyment and satisfaction from viewing the artwork.

Working with clay

Creating life with clay.

We typically spend more time working with clay during the warmer summer months. Clay is cool to touch and a bit messy, giving our hands the feeling of the cool dampness of the earth. This is a very different experience from working with watercolor paints. Clay doesn't flow: it requires more effort to effect a desired change in the medium's form. If you want something to happen with clay, you have to actively choose to change the shape. This draws on more of the individual's will, and even physical strength. Anna had such bad arthritis that she was left with very little ability to use her hands forcefully. In her case, we found a very pliable soft material at a craft store that was easy to form into different shapes. It dried with air and could be painted.

Initially, we make simple shapes from balls of clay: ovals, squares and pyramids. We enjoy our tactile interaction with the material. Simply by squishing the clay between fingers and thumb, beautiful waveforms can appear. One man, who was blind, got deep satisfaction from simply creating wave after wave after wave.

At another session, we may start with the same ball shape and find that birds, ducks, and seals emerge. From there, we have progressed to bears, dogs, cats, little families of animals, and human figures fishing or reading. We have also encountered dragons and other fierce looking creatures!

Pinch pots also come quite naturally from a round shape. This is an act of creation that it seems everyone was born instinctively knowing how to do. We hold the ball of clay in our hands with our thumbs on the top center of the ball. Slowly we press our thumbs down making the beginning of a small opening in the clay. Continuing to press our thumbs down, the hole deepens and widens as we press it against our fingers on the outside of the ball. It is transforming into a pot!

On another day, we may use rolling pins to flatten pieces of clay and decorate them with bits of different colored clay, textures, and stamps. Larger flattened pieces can become wall hangings, tiles, garden decorations, and coasters. Flattened pieces can also be rolled to make cylinders for pencil holders, candleholders, or vases. Sometimes, as a group project, we make a flat candleholder, and each participant creates their own little animal or bird or sea creature to be placed beside the candle.

Clay brings out something different in everyone. Lena's little houses, with flower boxes and round rugs, reflected her Swedish heritage. Sarah, who was deep into dementia, had difficulty with painting but was a natural with clay and made all kinds of dolls. Jean made duck after duck for many years, and then created people fishing. Betsy made angels and people reading books,

Ron made boats, and Arthur made perfect geometric shapes—each person on their own exploratory and artistic journey.

Ultimately, we will select some, but not all, of the pieces for firing, since the overall process is quite costly. Clay is not expensive; it is the glazing- and firing-related costs that add up. While it's nice to have a fired piece of clay to take home, there is still satisfaction to be gained from one left in its natural dried state. Red clay can be fun for the pots, since it dries with an old natural look.

Collage

Over the years, we discovered that tearing or cutting up our previously created, not-so-favorite watercolor paintings to make collages is a good use of their beautiful colors and shapes.

The facilitator provides scissors and demonstrates how to cut or tear the paper. Using a glue stick, pieces of varying shapes and sizes are attached to the same watercolor paper on which we paint. Sometimes the colorful pieces go off the edges of the paper's borders; sometimes they are curled or shaped into a 3D form. Again, you never know how individuals will respond to the artistic opportunity. Edna, for example, who didn't always seem to enjoy painting, stood for the entire hour happily working on her collage, completely unaware of her surroundings. If people are lower functioning, they may enjoy arranging precut shapes on the paper and be very pleased with their creation.

Time to kick back

As the participants finish their artistic projects, another transition begins. It is a pleasure to relax after the intense concentration and inward focus of our artistic work, and we shift to a collective outgoing attitude, talking and snacking before starting the movement portion of our day. Music usually plays softly while we refresh ourselves. It's a good time for social chitchat. Those who can move more easily offer each other cheese and crackers. The atmosphere is often jovial after the hard work of sustained inner attention.

We use our intuition to sense what the group is calling for and then attempt to balance the energy during the transition and movement time.

This is frequently a time when folks head to the restroom. Many of them have canes, walkers, wheelchairs, or are a little wobbly on their feet, so the facilitators tactfully accompany them down the hall to assure their safety.

Weather permitting, the doors or windows are opened to offer a breath of fresh air. While waiting for the entire group to reassemble in the open space, people admire the paintings on the wall or recognize their own work from a previous session. During this time, a very astute retired nurse often sees something she wants to change in one of her paintings.

This is a good time to assess the balance and energy of the group as a whole. If the energy is low and the participants seem tired, we might do a little self-care. We might massage ourselves, stretch, do deep-breathing exercises, or engage in other soothing, rhythmic movements. If the group is more energized, we will evaluate whether they would like to sing or if a livelier workout is called for. If the participants appear to be having good conversations, we may let the transition activities go on a little longer. Overall, we use our intuition to sense what the group is calling for and then attempt to balance the energy during the transition and movement time.

But soon we're complete again—individually, and as a group—and ready to begin the movement and exercise portion of the day.

Movement

*These are the same wooden poles Elderwise participants
have been using for more than 20 years!*

Exercise and movement activities are often times to let go a little. For those who have difficulty speaking, they can provide an avenue to recite words and speak loudly. We might offer them a short poem or song to repeat as they move, or we may match sounds to specific movements. Funny noises and groans are accepted and even encouraged—it feels good to be a little playful! But within the playfulness, we are conscious of the following components and goals:

- To let loose and shake out the limbs

- To employ yoga-style stretches and strengthening moves

- To move to the beat or rhythm of music for strengthening, posture, and joy

- To enhance the feeling of community

- To sing and to speak aloud

- To enhance circulation and awaken the whole body through breathing exercises, self-massage, and tapping

- To focus on deep and rhythmic breathing to attain an inner silence and restful feeling
- To use one's imagination through visualization

Movement is a terribly important part of life for all of us—but especially for those with dementia.

We first arrange the chairs with attention to spacing, making sure that the room is balanced and that everyone has room to stretch. Sometimes, we listen to music as we move our trunk and limbs, massage our arms and legs, feel the circulation moving throughout our bodies, and experience the space around us. We may reach up like a sunflower, using imagination to assist our movements; we may flutter kick our legs and imagine we're swimming in the ocean; or we may sing songs while flexing our hips or extending our knees. If we sing a marching song, it's a cue for people to lift their feet and swing their arms. It's like improv. You gather energy and see what people are responding to. It can be very freeing for all who participate.

We stand at the wall-mounted bars (chair backs can be used for this as well) and work the musculature that promotes our upright posture. We may put on some rousing music and dance, the joyous movement coming from within. Generally, we all feel expanded and larger than when we arrived.

At the close of the exercise session, we usually have a minute of quiet. We focus on our breath and encourage everyone to be aware of the feeling of well-being and warmth created by enhanced circulation throughout their bodies and the calm rhythm of their breathing. We follow this by sending thoughts and good wishes to others all over the world who, like ourselves, may be experiencing losses, disabilities, or other life challenges. It feels good to think of others. We may then end with a verse; something short and beautiful that can be repeated every time that can bring closure and a satisfying sense of completion to this portion of the day.

Movement is a terribly important part of life for all of us—but especially for those with dementia. For this reason, we encourage the participants' families to supplement our movement activities with walks outside, the use of gym facilities in their residential communities, their local YMCAs, or other exercise venues.

Lunch

A moment of connection before eating.

> *The Elderwise Way* is to share meals. We eat the same food at the same time and share the conversations that typically surround the breaking of bread together—the opposite of the us-versus-them mentality.

Following exercise, we often spend ten or fifteen minutes singing familiar songs as we wait for lunch to be put on the table. Lunch is a full part of the program, as important as artistic work, movement and discussion. If

Elderwise is providing the meal, we may hear the comforting sounds of chopping in the background, or the cook may bring in a beautiful beet for us to admire or even to paint.

Sometimes, because they are hungry and the smells of food being prepared are too enticing, people begin migrating to the dining table before exercise is officially over. One of the gifts of spirit-centered care is the lack of regimentation that permits such flexibility. People know that they will not be reprimanded for following their own rhythms and needs.

Breaking bread together can be sacred. Yet in most places where I have worked (including hospitals, skilled-nursing facilities, continuing-care retirement communities, and adult day centers), those being cared for and the staff members do not share meals. Rather, the two "groups" eat separate food at separate times in separate locations.

The Elderwise Way is to share meals. We eat the same food at the same time and share the conversations that typically surround the breaking of bread together—the opposite of the us-versus-them mentality. When everyone is seated, we begin our mealtime rituals. We start by passing out wipes or hand sanitizers, and then hold one another's hands while reciting a simple blessing: *Blessings on our lunch and peace be on the earth.* Then it becomes quiet again as we all dig in. We share the smells and sight of the food, we pass around the butter or other condiments, and we enjoy the adventure of trying new and different foods. We eat grains that some of our participants have never heard of before, like quinoa and millet; we have lots of green and other brightly colored fresh vegetables; tofu, and such specialties as beet soup seasoned with fresh basil. The tastes are delicious, especially when shared in community.

When lunch is prepared in a facility, rather than cooking it ourselves, we have less control over the beauty of the food, but it is enjoyed just the same. Whether cooked ourselves or by others, we will not all always like every aspect of the food. It may be too salty or lukewarm. Good-humored comments may be made, and food may or may not be completely eaten, but the meal and company are enjoyed and we do our best to accept what is given graciously.

After-lunch discussion

Time to talk; time to listen.

After we've enjoyed some good, nutritious food and the table has been cleared, we pour tea into ceramic teacups and pass around dessert. As we lean back in our seats, the focus is again shifted: The facilitator introduces an idea or a topic and, with a thought-provoking question, the stage is set for group discussion. Often the discussion topic comes from the facilitator's personal experience; perhaps an event has occurred that has caused her to wonder about something. Or the question might be inspired by a magazine article, a research study, or ideas pertaining to aging or philosophy.

These topics may, but frequently don't, demand sharp memories of the past; usually they are things that can be reflected upon in the moment. *What are things that make you happy? What nourishes you? What do you fear about growing older? Would you like to share something about a special relationship?* One doesn't just start with a question; there is a build-up to it, a story-telling or experience-sharing that leads the participants to engage with the subject.

In a recent discussion, we talked about a young man who was about to graduate from a Seattle high school. There was a photo of him in the *Seattle Times,* taken at the local annual Folklife Festival: he was text messaging on his cell phone. What made this of interest to the *Seattle Times* journalist was the fact that the young man came from a tribe in South America whose village is only accessible by an eight-hour boat ride. The young man was to return to his tribe that summer and, perhaps, would someday take on a leadership role. The reporter asked him if he would have difficulty adjusting back to his tribal way of life. His answer was that he would not miss the pace of life here in Seattle.

At this point, the facilitator asked the following questions: *What do you think about the pace of life in the city these days? With cell phones, text messaging, computers, crowded highways, and complicated tax forms, do you ever have a desire to live in a place where the pace of life is slower? Are there ways to live in a city such as Seattle and not get caught up in the rapid pace of life?*

We live in a society that doesn't usually slow down in order for the voices of the frail elder to be heard. If we can listen more deeply to what they have to say, we can really see them, know more who they are, and learn from them.

Each person at the table—participants, staff, and visitors as well—has a chance to respond fully to the question. When one person is speaking, all other conversation stops and we focus on what is being said. Everyone at the table may bring a different insight to the question or hold a different point of view. The facilitator listens attentively and decides if and when support is needed: rephrasing a question; assisting a participant to share their thoughts; repeating the gist of a conversation in order for all to hear and understand; drawing meaning out of a group of expressed thoughts and responses. One day, a participant in our group discussion took a long time to articulate her opinion. I was touched to the point of tears by the quiet patience of the others as they listened intently, making sure that they understood what she wanted to communicate.

We live in a society that doesn't usually slow down in order for the voices of the frail elder to be heard. If we can listen more deeply to what they have to say, we can really see them, know more who they are, and learn from them. It can be particularly challenging for family members to do this. This is one reason why interactions with others, whether at a formal program like Elderwise or at a community center, are so important. At whatever age we are, there is little that is more precious than to be heard, seen, and valued. At Elderwise, we are very careful not to interrupt. We make sure space is given for each person to finish their thought. In the hearing is the valuing.

Nancy says her daughter doesn't understand her. "She thinks I'm dumb," she tells the group. Despite her memory loss, she lives alone in the house that has been her home for decades. "How can I explain to her that even though I have difficulty with practical things, that doesn't mean I don't also have a certain kind of wisdom, the kind that comes from experiencing so much every day for so many years? All she focuses on is that I forgot to turn off the stove, and fall now and then."

Ella enjoys the companionship around the table. She likes that we talk about important things. Often, she can't remember what happened a minute ago, and while she couldn't tell you the specifics of yesterday's discussion—or even today's conversation—she understands that we talk about important and meaningful topics. It's hard to know what is happening inside cognitively, but it is clear that there are reverberations resonating in her being. She feels better and fuller since she started coming to Elderwise.

And as Darlene said one day, "I really enjoy hearing what others have to say. It helps me feel less isolated. It's so good just to be able to talk about important subjects. I am so glad to have this place where time slows down enough for me to be able to express my deeper thoughts and where I can listen to other people's."

A good cup of tea and good feelings from a meaningful discussion are served up daily at the Elderwise table.

The day concludes

Appreciating the day's creations.

When the discussion group is brought to a close, we thank everyone for their participation and start to get them ready to go home. We send them off with the hope that each is full with the satisfaction of having had a positive and meaningful day, a day that has called upon all aspects of who they are as human beings, a day that has called upon us to stretch in bodies and minds, and recognize the fullness of our spirit that can express itself as completely as ever.

CHAPTER FOUR:

The Concept of Wholeness

*Feeling the quiet support of each other's presence
while deeply engaged with one's own creativity.*

What makes us whole?

Mentally envision the youngest person you know. Now see the oldest, and the array of people at various ages in between. Then ask yourself the following questions:

- Are you whole if you are a baby?

- Are you whole if you are a toddler?

- Are you whole if you are a teenager?

- Are you whole if you are a person with an amputation? Multiple sclerosis? Mental illness?

- Are you whole if you are one hundred and five years old?

• Are you whole if you have dementia?

Different considerations and rationales emerge when addressing these questions. A baby doesn't have full brain-cell connectivity; a toddler doesn't have a full level of motor control or self-regulation; a teenager doesn't have a fully developed frontal cortex. Yet we have a societal understanding that individuals in these age groups are whole, even though not fully developed, either mentally or physically.

We also have a general societal understanding that if someone has had an amputation of a body part, the personhood, the *Who are you?* of that individual, their essence, remains intact. But when a disease state affects the brain, such as in Parkinson's or schizophrenia, the question hits closer to home and we may not be as clear in our answers. Even more so with dementia: As brain function—the ability to think and remember—progressively declines, how then do we answer the question, *Is this person whole?*

The Elderwise answer to all of these questions is a resounding Yes! At the core of who one is, one is whole. I am not saying that problems with the body or brain are not losses. A broken leg is a loss; an amputation is a loss; and dementia is an even bigger loss because it gets closer to one's essence, or what one identifies as I/me/myself. But we are more than our bodies and more than our brains. The core or essence of who we are is whole, always.

When I speak with someone,
I speak to the whole, the depth,
of who that person is.
I am not speaking to a broken leg,
or an amputation, or dementia:
I am speaking to the wholeness of the other.

This is an invaluable attitude to hold. When I speak with someone, I speak to the whole, the depth, of who that person is. I am not speaking to a broken leg, or an amputation, or dementia: I am speaking to the wholeness of the other.

We are born, we live, and we die. During our lifetimes, our bodies develop and our brains develop. Inevitably, we have problems with those bodies, brains, or both. While we don't all get dementia, many of us will have cognitive loss of some sort. Part of my life's work is to bring some normalizing to what happens to our minds as well as our bodies as we age. We are used to thinking of such losses as being destructive of a person's essence, but in my experience, this has nothing to do with *who* anyone is as a person, any more than losing a limb or an organ changes the essence of who we are.

Eastern philosophy, which I have studied for many decades, has some concepts that, for those of us who grew up in the west, are hard to take in. The question of *Who am I?* is one of them. We are so identified with our bodies—we think *that* is who we are. After thirty years of Vedanta teachings—and the death of my daughter—I have begun to make at least a tiny bit of headway in understanding a different idea: *We are not our bodies.* We can do our best to keep them strong, youthful-looking and attractive. We can cover them in cool clothing or colorfully adorn them. Yet they do not equal who we are—rather, our bodies are a wonderful tool in which to explore the world. Even as Westerners, though we may not articulate this very often, we have a sense, an understanding, that if you have a broken leg, you are still you, or if your gall bladder is removed, you haven't lost the "you" part of you. The question is, how far can we go with this? Are you still you if you are a quadriplegic or lose the power of speech?

Going deeper: *Are we our senses?* The information we gain by the ability to see, hear, smell, taste, and touch helps us to understand our world. We use this knowledge, but the ability to see is not who we are. What does it mean if your hearing doesn't work? What if you lose your sight? We know our senses become less sensitive with age. *Do we also become less with age* as our senses diminish? Are we dense because we can't hear, or ignorant because we can't see? A person who has these losses is often treated this way but inside knows better, and even most in Western society can understand that a blind person is no less whole…but can we go further still?

Mind does not equal brain

Older adults often say to me, "I don't feel old; I don't feel different inside." That's because *the essence of who we are doesn't change.* It does not age. My mother-in-law no longer remembers who I am. But when I sit with her and she holds my hand, we feel each other's essence. Her physical and mental tools don't work the way they used to, which, of course, is a loss. But our time together is no less valuable because she won't remember it after I've gone. Sometimes, at the end of our visit and I am heading home, I realize that I am happier than when I came. This is the gift of connecting on a heart level and not being troubled by the brain's limitations.

In Eastern philosophy, the brain and the mind are considered to be different things. The brain is *the tool you utilize* for thinking, for learning, for analyzing, for decision-making, whereas the mind, in that concept, is *closer to the essence* of who you are. The mind is not located in the brain, any more than what we see is located in our eyes. The mind is not damaged when the brain is damaged; it has simply lost the vehicle through which it can express itself in the world.

This concept that mind does not equal brain is a hard one for Westerners to grasp. Brain is part of the physical body; it is the finest part of that body and our tool for thinking. When the brain is injured or diseased or not functioning well, it is a great loss, because it diminishes our ability to learn optimally. But it does not alter the essence of who we are. Even if you have lost some brainpower, who you are remains. Even, you have not lost your mind.

My mother-in-law no longer remembers who I am. But when I sit with her and she holds my hand, we feel each other's essence. Her physical and mental tools don't work the way they used to, which, of course, is a loss. But our time together is no less valuable because she won't remember it after I've gone.

This is because the depth of who we are—the soul, the Self, the ultimate reality, ultimate truth, joy or love itself—does not change, whatever the outer conditions. It is not affected by illness or disease. This is our essence.

Sometimes, as a way to remind myself of this, I like to imagine someone wearing different layers of clothing—a brown coat, say, covers a red jacket and, under that, a blue turtle-neck sweater. When I am with that person, I see the coat and the jacket and I may even have some opinion about them. Perhaps I like the color combination, or perhaps I don't. Perhaps I see the sweater and observe its various qualities: how it's made, its texture. But when I speak to that person, I do my best to speak to *who that person is*, not to the coat or the jacket or the sweater. In the same way, I may see that someone has had a stroke or observe that they seem confused, but I do my best to speak to the essence of that person—not to the stroke or to the dementia or to whatever else I may discern from outside appearances.

The Elderwise Way. This invaluable *concept of wholeness* informs our work. It is central to the *spirit-centered model of care,* in which we treat all persons with the respect and reverence that acknowledges who the individual is at the very depth of their being. And that person—no matter what their age or level of function—will understand that you see them, that you see who they really are, and they will feel the depth of that respect and the dignity with which they are being perceived and addressed.

CHAPTER FIVE:

The Foundation of Spirit-Centered Care

The foundation of spirit-centered
care is a profound recognition that
each person's essence is immutable,
regardless of the physical or cognitive
changes they may go through
in their lifetime.

The foundation of spirit-centered care is a profound recognition that each person's essence is immutable, regardless of the physical or cognitive changes they may go through in their lifetime.

We believe that as long as we are going deeply into honoring the wholeness of each person, why not go all the way, and address and work with each unique individual from that perspective? Everything we do at Elderwise acknowledges and attends to the wholeness of individuals. When considering programming, we think about the entirety of a person: body, mind, and spirit. We recognize that while a person may have experienced physical, social, emotional, or cognitive changes, *the essence of who they are remains the same.* And we recognize that, in the deepest sense, *we are all equal.* This is the foundation of the Elderwise philosophy. It has many implications for every moment-to-moment interaction, whether in a professional environment like Elderwise or in one's personal realm.

There are five practices that are necessary for fostering and carrying out the Elderwise philosophy of spirit-centered care:

- Recognizing and working from one's own essence

- A recognition of the essence of others

- A deep respect for our equality, no matter our present condition

- An understanding that roles can instantly change (the us-versus-them phenomenon)

- Active development of deep listening

Fostering these five attitudes enriches our own spiritual lives and enlivens our work with those in our care, especially the frail elder.

Recognizing one's own essence

What do we mean by *essence?* What comes to mind when we talk about the *essence* of something? Is it the inherent, fundamental property that identifies something as itself? Is it the unchanging nature of something? The Oxford English Dictionary defines it as, "The intrinsic nature or indispensable quality of something, especially something abstract, which determines its character." Another way to say it is that essence is the thing without which something would not be itself.

Sometimes, when pondering the question of essence, I use the image of a woman layered in a thousand cloaks (I seem to like images that involve many layers of clothing!). What are the many kinds of cloaks that she is wearing? Perhaps a sweater of personality, a scarf of behavior, a hat of culture, a coat of character, a pair of earrings of quirks, and a vest of style. If these cloaks and more are peeled off, layer by layer, what is left—and I don't mean the body— is the essence of a person.

In the martial art of Aikido, for example, one is taught to be aware of and move from one's center, or essence. Whether moving to one side or another, quickly forward or gracefully backwards, one is always in tune with one's own center. And after the training session is over, ideally the practice is carried off the mat and out into the world, as one maintains an awareness of that center while moving through the day.

If you work in this way, your actions will be in alignment with your essential wholeness, and your work will naturally become a life-affirming spiritual practice, bringing joy, depth, and meaning to whatever you do.

Whether in a family, a workplace, or any other situation or setting, deliberately operating from your own essence is a profoundly beneficial approach to you and all with whom you come into contact. It means that you work from the deepest part of yourself, that central truth of your being. This truth is actually the same for all of us, even if we each see it in our own way, even if we each identify it differently.

Recognizing the essence of others

The reason we care about this word, essence, is because it is the source of deep respect, for self and others. I know that it is there in every human being, regardless of what the outward appearance might demonstrate. In some, it may be harder to access and recognize. If I am with somebody that has memory loss, I might not have a deep respect for the way they repeat the same questions over and over. However, if I know, in my heart of hearts, that underneath that outward appearance, their essence remains unchanged, respect comes naturally, though not necessarily effortlessly. There are days at Elderwise when I am really challenged to remember this, days when I get caught up in the exhaustion of the repetitive, circular conversations, and the anxiety some people display. It takes a toll on me and it takes away from the flow of the day for everyone. I have to utilize all the skills I have developed over the years to bring us back to center. It is when I am able to look through the eyes of my own essence that I can more easily find, recognize, acknowledge, and connect with the intrinsic essence of another.

Of course I have an awareness of the other's various outer cloaks, be they emotional or physical garments. Whether I am being confronted by depression, agitation, and dementia, or politeness, manners, and thoughtfulness, my aim is to speak to the essence and wholeness of another human being as much as possible.

In Asian cultures, people frequently acknowledge each other with hands pressed together and head bowed, saying the Sanskrit word *Namaste (The spirit in me honors the spirit in you)*. This gesture, which has now become familiar in the West as well, indicates that the person is recognizing the deepest part, or essence, of the other. Imparted in this simple gesture is a valuable attitude: While your cloaks may be amusing, annoying, entertaining, enriching or frustrating, as I bow, I see and acknowledge who you really are; from my humblest, deepest center, I honor and acknowledge you.

The experience of equality

The depth of one person's essence is no greater or lesser than the depth of another person's essence. In this way, essence is a great equalizer. This recognition of essence is the basis of that which fosters the sense of equality among the participants and staff around the table. But what does equality really mean in the context of caring for and about our elders? How do we create an environment that fosters the ongoing growth of the whole individual within the frail-elder community? What equality-based attitudes might foster an individual's sense of wholeness and continuity as their body and brain experiences the effects of aging and disease?

The cloaks people wear may be different; we all take on different roles. But whether one is a supervisor or a supervisee, a resident or a visitor, a doctor or a patient, a caregiver or a care receiver, the essence of one person is not better or worse than that of another. The essence of all people has the same value. Despite a broken leg, a mental illness, or dementia, or even criminal or immoral actions, each person's essence has the same worth. In Vedanta, an Eastern philosophy, it is said that the essence of each person is the same, but in some persons it is more manifest than in others.[2] We all know that there are certain people we enjoy being around more than others, and that this does not depend on the person's social or economic status. There are those whose company we seek—and others whom we avoid—because of something ineffable that emanates from them.

The Elderwise program uses this idea that our essences are equal to foster the feeling that all those gathered at our table are equally valuable.

Awareness of the us-versus-them phenomenon

Roles can change in a split second, a reminder that we should not become too identified with the role (or cloak) we wear, or in the respect, benefits, perks— or lack thereof—that go with the role. This was forcefully demonstrated to me some months ago when I hit the pavement and broke bones in both my arm and my foot. I went from being fully independent and active to being quite dependent on the ministrations of others. It is an experience that helped me anew to fully appreciate the fluidity of these role changes. I call this the "us-versus-them" phenomenon, one that is too frequently seen in residential living and care facilities where big divides exist between residents or patients and the professional caregivers, healthcare providers, and management.

---

2 *The Gospel of Sri Ramakrishna* Copyright © 1942 by Swami Nikhilananda 7th printing 1984 pg. 211

Whether one is a resident in a nursing home needing continuous care, or whether one is the paid caregiver, each person has the same value. It also does not mean that the situation will remain as it is. It is important to be aware that, at any moment, one's own situation can suddenly change, as one fall changed mine. Doctors can suddenly have a heart attack and immediately find themselves in a passive, dependent capacity, the situation perhaps even calling for the original care receiver to provide CPR! Or a care receiver can become an active caregiver within the course of one day, as when a person, having just recovered from total knee replacement, goes home to care for a spouse with Alzheimer's disease.

Here, the attitude to foster is the awareness that things can and will change. It may appear that you are at the top of your game, but roles are transient and circumstances can shift in an instant. It is helpful to understand that there is not too much difference between any of us, even after the usual stratifying of occupational or family roles. Understanding the fragile nature of life can be a humbling—and helpful—reminder that we are all in the same boat.

Deep listening

There is nothing more validating or empowering than to be listened to and understood. Rachel Naomi Remen, author, physician, and healer, elucidates deep listening so beautifully in her story, "To Be Seen by the Heart," from her book *Kitchen Table Wisdom.*

Remen begins her story of herself as a young girl with the words, "When we are seen by the heart we are seen for who we are." She describes how she felt truly seen by her godfather when, moments before his death, he gently reached out his old hand towards her. When I read this story, I can feel the effort it must have taken him, in those last moments, to make contact with this child. I can see his gnarled hand clasping her small child's one, as with his whole self he whispered her name, "Rachel," as he "met" her deeply for the first time. Even though she was a very young child of three, she still recalls that experience of being seen from the heart.

Though Rachel's mother was horrified that the old man died in her daughter's presence, from Rachel's point of view she, the young girl, had received a wonderful gift—the gift of being truly seen by another.

> # One cannot overestimate the power of deep listening: listening with attention and an open heart.

There is no greater gift than to be seen in this way. It is especially important for people with memory loss to be really seen: they know, whether they are able to express the feeling in words or not, that their existence is being recognized and acknowledged by another. It is a way to reach into their deep isolation and help ease their loneliness and fear.

Deep listening comes from a place of balance and centeredness. From this place of calm, we can see the other in front of us, share with them and love them, recognizing empathetically their wholeness and their woundedness. We can give the gift of time, of listening, and of encouragement. The underlying message is that of *Namaste*: The spirit in me honors the spirit in you.

One cannot overestimate the power of deep listening: listening with attention and an open heart. In the course of our daily lives, we have many opportunities to be together and share with one another. But often the time needed for deep listening is not readily available. Too frequently in our fast-paced world, we undervalue the therapeutic importance of truly listening—and truly being heard. When you add dementia to the picture, it can be especially time-consuming to understand someone who may have difficulty finding words or formulating thoughts.

If we can learn to quiet our own minds enough to fully "take in" another, to listen deeply, we will be giving—and receiving—one of life's greatest gifts. How marvelous to be truly together with another person: to see and to hear; to be seen and to be heard. It is this kind of time that the Elderwise approach cultivates.

CHAPTER SIX:

The Practice of Spirit-Centered Care

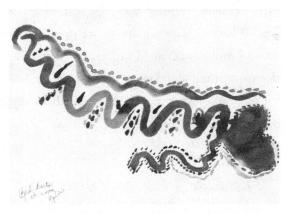

Can we support the frail elder in growing spiritually, even at this stage of their lives? And, if so, how do we do it? Spirit-centered care is the approach we use in the Elderwise program because it fosters our goal of helping each person—participant and facilitator alike—become more open, more loving, more willing to try new things, more confident, more joyful, more broad-minded, and more expansive. We also want them to have a really good time!

Spirit-centered care is the approach we use in the Elderwise program because it fosters our goal of helping each person—participant and facilitator alike—become more open, more loving, more willing to try new things, more confident, more joyful, more broad-minded, and more expansive.

Spiritual health

Thanks to the pioneering work of psychologist Erik Erikson, we no longer think of human development as being complete when one reaches adulthood. Rather, we embrace the exciting possibility—as well as the challenging responsibility—that we continue to grow and learn until we die. Unless one is a saint or a sage, we don't get to say, *Okay, I'm done now*, at some arbitrary time in our lives. Whatever stage we are at, we need to continue to take responsibility for our own growth and learning; yet, if another person needs support in order to continue developing as they age, we would like to be able to offer that support—just as we would provide that individual with the opportunity to continue walking with the use of a cane.

> *The Elderwise Way* provides an environment in which people can claim their full essence, and know that if they do not remember a word or need help with expressing an idea, they are not less than whole.

Sometimes young children look at us with eyes that seem to see right through to our soul. Perhaps they are not fooled by outer appearances but understand our depth. *The Elderwise Way* provides an environment in which people can claim their full essence, and know that if they do not remember a word or need help with expressing an idea, they are not less than whole.

In retirement communities, a person's center or core is often neglected. There are parties for Halloween, or Olympic Games for fun; there are Happy Hours with wine and peanuts—but what about focusing and valuing peace of mind? What about talking about aging and death and life's other big questions, rather than filling the hours with distractions? Distractions from the work of aging—that it is becoming time to complete any last tasks prior to our death, that we need to face our own mortality. I do know of much meaningful spiritual care going on in communities around the country, but it is not generally the primary focus it could be.

I consider the ability to go inward and be at peace to be a fundamental element of spiritual health and well-being. Having a peaceful death with a sense of life completion is so important.

The Elderwise approach to supporting spiritual well-being

I consider the ability to go inward and be at peace to be a fundamental element of spiritual health and well-being. Having a peaceful death with a sense of life completion is so important. A person considered to be a frail elder by our definition may experience grumpiness, sadness, fear, anger, and loneliness, all of which are understandable feelings given the physical, social, and mental losses so often experienced with aging and, even more so, with aging and dementia. What kind of support is called for when thinking about spiritual health for the frail elder?

One of the ways we answer this question at Elderwise is to offer participants a variety of opportunities for personal or spiritual growth.

Since older adults are all too often painfully aware of how they can't contribute any more, having opportunities to make even a small difference to someone else's day—by listening, smiling, or sharing good humor—helps them experience themselves as still having value in the world. Sweeping, planting, clearing the table, folding napkins—all these things contribute to the general well-being of one's environment, whether it is family, a residential community, or any other social setting.

Another way to stimulate our best selves is by discussing and reflecting on topics such as gratitude, love, values, what we've learned in our lifetimes. This is the time that each person can reflect on important ideas such as, *What is my truth, what do I fundamentally believe, what are my values?* The questions we ask are designed to draw out these core beliefs from each individual. Sometimes there is a basket on the table from which each participant pulls out a slip of paper with a word on it: Aging, Truth, Beauty, Love, Nature, Courage, Strength, and so on. For lower cognition level groups, we might start with a question about Nature, something that could be as simple as, *How do you love Nature?* Or even, *Are you a person that loves Nature?* From such a simple starting point, we have had discussions of surprising depth, in which we get to know each other more intimately.

Another way to offer opportunities for spiritual connection is to intersperse the day with rituals, such as holding hands for a moment of grace before a shared meal, reading a poem or lighting a candle before beginning our artistic work. Such small, simple gestures are powerful connectors to our essence. If someone from the group has passed away, or no longer is able to come, we acknowledge that with some kind of a ritual, such as lighting a special candle, dedicating a special vase of flowers to their memory, passing their picture around. This last is especially helpful to those for whom memory is a major issue. Seeing the image of the one who is gone is often a jog to their memories.

At Elderwise, we also have supported quiet time, but not the kind of quiet that comes when people are just spacing out. These are moments of mindful silence. When we finish our exercise, I often ask people to be quiet for one minute. Our circulatory systems have been stimulated and I will say, *Close your eyes. Be quiet and feel the sense of well-being that is moving through your body.* I might also encourage consciously choosing to focus on the love in our hearts, starting with love for ourselves and then moving that out to include others in the circle, in the room, and then beyond. We send love to those we know and those we don't know, sometimes focusing on unknown others who may be in similar situations in other parts of the world.

The opportunities to create activities that touch the heart and open the doors to our deeper selves are endless.

Older models of caring for those with dementia

These days, the concept of *person-centered care* is generally accepted in the long-term care community. This is a huge improvement over *body-centered care*, which considers the person primarily as a body that must be bathed, fed, clothed, and medically treated. And it is miles above and beyond *facility-centered care*, which first and foremost considers organizational benefits and staff schedules in caring for those bodies.

Person-centered care makes the individual, and their preferences, the primary concern. What time someone might want to get up; what that person might like for breakfast and even if they want to eat breakfast at all—these are the kinds of things that are considered in person-centered care. In addition, individuals are given choices regarding their lifestyle, activities, and social opportunities. It is a huge progressive step that begins to acknowledge the *who* of a person as well as the *what*. This supports continuity within their life as they move into this new stage. It is so important to tie the existence of a person, who may be living in a retirement community or another supported living circumstance, to the life they led when they were younger and healthier by keeping the fabric of their lives as intact as possible.

What is so significant about person-centered care is that it moves professional care towards recognizing *the importance of the essence of who a person really is.* Most people who practice person-centered care believe that this includes the spiritual aspect: "As important as the body is, the holistic triad of body-mind-spirit cannot be overemphasized."[3]

---

3 Richard H. Savel, MD, and Cindy L. Munro, RN, PhD, ANP, *The Importance of Spirituality in Patient-Centered Care* ©2014 American Association of Critical-Care Nurses, http://ajcc.aacnjournals.org/content/23/4/276.full (accessed October 17, 2019)

Spirit-Centered Care

The Elderwise philosophy and practice takes person-centered care one step further, to what we call spirit-centered care: the conscious recognition and honoring of one's own essence and that of others. This concept is the foundation of all our work. Spirit-centered care includes upholding the principles we explored earlier: a deep respect for the experience of equality; maintaining an awareness of the us-versus-them phenomenon; and deep listening. These principles inspire, motivate and propel everyone connected with *The Elderwise Way*. Spirit-centeredness is the underpinning of the many intangibles that make the Elderwise approach so exceptional.

Spirit-centeredness is the underpinning of the many intangibles that make the Elderwise approach so exceptional.

Elderwise is not a clinical setting. It is a human setting. When a person enters, we aim to touch the depth of their essence, to support them in experiencing their own wholeness. Yes, they may wear cloaks of poor balance, forgetfulness, or painful joints—we are all decorated differently. But whatever their current decoration, nothing is wrong with their essence. I believe that people, whatever their cognitive condition, recognize when they are being treated with this level of respect.

While one's actions may differ only slightly when one carries this attitude, I believe this respect is felt in all interactions in subtle and important ways. Experience supports this belief; it is what I have witnessed in the Elderwise environment. We help participants understand that, in their core, they aren't *less than*, whatever their intellectual losses. Some understand that those losses are impacting them, yet being valued in this way causes them to sit up a little straighter and express themselves with more confidence as they share their opinions, paint or joke around.

The Elderwise philosophy aims to counteract the everyday reality that often frail elders—and especially those with declining senses or reduced cognition—isolate themselves because of an inability to get out, an inability to hear or see clearly, or an inability to understand what's going on. They feel that it's safer and more comfortable to stay home, maybe even to sleep or to shut down by watching endless hours of television. This isolating experience is self-perpetuating: it can make one more closed, fearful, and unwilling to try new things. Instead, by acknowledging the essence of each person and treating them with a deep respect, people are drawn out of their isolation and feel free to express themselves as fully as possible. It's amazing what happens when folks don't feel limited by the judgments of others!

By acknowledging the essence of each person and treating them with a deep respect, people are drawn out of their isolation and feel free to express themselves as fully as possible.

IT'S ALL GOOD

by *David Leek*

Nature has provided me with
Her own celebratory plaque.
It is white and, I believe, quite pure.
It fills my mind,
In a manner of speaking.

I had not previously heard
The mysterious and alliterative term.
"Pre-senile dementia."

I must admit, it has a certain authoritative ring.
Medical titles usually do
And this one is quite official sounding.

It tells the story of a slow, crustaceous process,
Sort of like the accretion of silt
At the bend of a river
Where movement is diminished
And small bits of detritus,
No longer carried forward with enough motion,
Begin to drift downward
Until they settle, softly, at the bottom.
Memory, like the drifting silt,
Becomes inert.

But, it is a slow process.
And I am not yet entirely transformed
From flowing river to fen.

Sometimes I feel frightened
By the future I imagine.
But, really, my fears of what may come
Are quite likely to be forgotten
Once the process is complete.

And, as I write this
I hold tightly to my secret weapon,
My willingness to live now, in this moment,
With its ever-changing kaleidoscope
Of texture, temperature, sound
And every other sense that brings me
The wonderful awareness of living.

CHAPTER SEVEN:

Aging and the Senses

The experience of dementia
challenges everyone involved
to stretch and expand in new ways.

Our changing relationship with the senses

The experience of dementia challenges everyone involved to stretch and
expand in new ways. Old modes of being may now feel closed off. The task is
to discover new approaches—or modify existing routes—to relating to others, to one's self, and to the world. Just as when vision is lost or impaired and
we offer other sensory modes (such as focusing on touch or sound) to stimulate engagement with the world, we can use alternative approaches to reach a

person with dementia. These alternate "ways in" comprise a path to offering enrichment that reaches the depths of a person's wholeness, stimulating all parts of who they are.

We know that the body declines with age. We can hope that along the way we have sufficiently developed our inner selves so that, as the body declines, our psychological and spiritual selves do not decline as well. If we remain firmly attached to our previous physical and cognitive functionality, our spirits and psyches may be dragged down along with the declining body. With maturity and spiritual practice, however, we can, as we saw in Chapter Four, begin to separate the mind from its attachment to the body and brain. This way, even as we physically decline, we can continue to grow and expand spiritually. Though not an easy task, my goal, as I age, is to increasingly identify with my spirit, rather than this body and brain that are presenting new challenges to me all the time.

When we are young, the senses are difficult to ignore—they are aglow with new stimuli and activity, and they demand our attention, practically dragging us through our days. But the wisdom of older age—along with weakening physical energy and depleted hormones— can shine light on the senses. Their power over us is less strong. We can observe them and better understand that they do not own us. We know that we don't want our senses to be leading our lives. *We* want to be leading our lives.

The Elderwise Way. We all have different temperaments and we all use our senses differently. With age, some love to quietly look out the window; others need more activity and engagement, though not necessarily to be entertained. When working with the frail elder, we should not rate quality of life by the number of activities someone participates in. Rather, we should be more interested in the whole person and their peace of mind. We can strive to create an environment in which one may seek peace with the world and peace within one's self. Among the ways we do this is by deepening our understanding of the senses and how they impact our experience of the world.

The concept of the twelve senses

Typically, we learn about five senses: touch, vision, smell, taste, and hearing, possibly with the addition of a sixth sense, one which we might call *intuition*. A different concept—that of twelve senses—originated with Rudolf Steiner, an Austrian philosopher, whose work bridged the late nineteenth and early twentieth centuries. The twelve senses are separated into three groups: the physical senses, the emotional or feeling senses, and the spiritual senses.

While considering twelve senses instead of six may seem far-fetched, it isn't really such a strange approach if you think about all the various ways by which we gain information about the world and ourselves. I am offering this concept here as another framework with which we can reach people living with memory loss—or anyone else, for that matter. I have taught this to groups where memory loss was not the issue. One woman, on her way out from such a group, made a point of stopping and expressing her appreciation for this new tool: "It's given me a new way of reflecting on the balance of these aspects in my own life."

Over the years, I have found that this approach provides a rich foundation from which we can look at the whole person. It also provides a lens that helps us discover a wider variety of beneficial enrichment activities. Thinking about programming in this manner allows for the promise of growth and ensures that we keep in mind the importance of nourishing the whole person. It also helps us to understand where an individual might need some targeted support.

Whether we're looking at six or twelve senses, it's clear that they are interdependent. When you eat, for example, you experience taste, vision, smell, temperature, and so on. And though the twelve senses are presented in categories (physical, emotional, spiritual), that is not to say that one sense is more important than any other. Building on each other, all of them can provide an opportunity for personal growth. Still, these classifications can enrich our understanding of how we relate to the world.

Transforming our relationship with the senses

Our journey is from a strong sensory experience to more refinement as we age. Our challenge is to discover how to use the senses for personal growth and for making progress on that journey. As we age, our physical senses and abilities decline, sometimes to the point where getting out of a chair unassisted is a challenge. But the real challenge is not to be disheartened and depressed because we can't do things. Rather, our aim is to deepen our appreciation for the internal abilities and development that we are still able to realize. Outwardly, I may not balance on my legs so well any more, but inside, I *feel* balanced. Outwardly, I'm not as strong as I once was, but inwardly, I *am* strong.

In this manner, our relationship with the senses becomes transformed. And, as we become less dependent on the body and more reliant on our inner life, the power that the senses have over us is reduced.

THE GOD OF SMALL THINGS

by *David Leek*

The god of small things is my friend.
I breathe, occasionally remembering
To notice the soft deflation and inflation
Of my accordion lungs;

Slow, enjoyable exhaling, with the expectation
Of the incoming wave that comes
On its own,
Until, one day
It won't.

I am thinking of my daughter,
Who lives now far away.
I remember that I, too,
Left home, moved far away
And felt new and strong;
Beginning the long meal of my life,
Bite by bite, tasting chewing, never questioning
My pursuit of each moment.

There is a softness in me
That I greatly appreciate.
It reflects my wish to be carefully held,
Warmly explored by a thoughtful and sympathetic friend.

Which, I suppose, is why I am attentive to others.
I don't sing; I can't dance,
But I listen,
And find beauty in the tender center of hope
That everyone seems to carry,
And few care to explore.

CHAPTER EIGHT:

The Four Physical Senses

Tactile engagement with the centerpiece.

The four physical senses refer to the sense of touch, life, balance, and movement. They have to do with becoming aware of our own physical bodies—how is it that "I" am in this body, separate from "you"? How does this body operate and how can I gain mastery over it?

Touch

With touch, we begin our journey of learning about the world around us. It is with this sense that we come to understand that we are distinctly different from others. Through the sense of touch, we gain awareness of our body. Bumping up against objects, we learn where our bodies stop and where the rest of the world begins. Without this experience of *self*, we cannot have the experience of *other* as separate from ourselves.

We come into this world without such a sense of self. Our nine months held in the safety of the womb are ended suddenly. While we come to appreciate our physical independence, there remains a lingering sadness in our bodily isolation. On some perceptual level, we may feel the *loss of one-ness*—that we somehow got separated from the whole—and now must use all our wits and resources to find our way home. That's why touch can be filled with such longing. We yearn for it to bring us that feeling of oneness again, that lost feeling of safety and intimacy but, at best, we learn that such union is only temporary.

This does not diminish the importance of the experience of genuine physical communication, whether it is with a human being or a tree. With true and honest touch, a person begins to understand the very nature of the touched object and learns the importance of having respect for all things. The opposite is true as well.

A few years ago, walking on a beach in British Columbia, I came upon a truly disturbing scene. Two sets of parents were sitting on a log, chatting peacefully. On the beach below them, not more than six feet away, their children were running around in a circle, holding sticks in their hands and hitting something in the center of that circle. As I got closer, I could see that it was the body of a large sea mammal, maybe a walrus, maybe a big seal.

This was a very public area in front of a hotel. Other people were on the beach and the boardwalk. The kids were not doing something in secret. They weren't hiding their actions. What's the harm? I'm sure they thought. This animal is dead. Who cares?

I cared. I looked at the parents, stunned that they weren't saying anything to stop their children. But they went on chatting unconcernedly, as the kids kept laughing and beating the corpse. I don't typically intervene with other people's children, especially when I don't know them. But my horror overtook my reserve and I yelled out to the kids, "What are you doing?" They looked at me in blank surprise. "You have to have respect," I said. "This animal is about the size of a person. Would you do this to a human body? This was a living being that recently died. You have to have respect for it."

At this point, the parents, perhaps to placate this shouting woman, told them to stop. I am not under any illusion that my interference made a big change—this isn't something you learn on a one-off—but I hope that at least one of them thinks a little more deeply about their relationship with the world around them.

When we have experiences of deep respect for everything, whether animate or inanimate, our ability to empathize is fostered—we are prepared to walk a mile in another person's shoes. Similarly, we come to understand that we, too, impart a vibration to everything—and anyone—we touch. Think of being in a church: You can feel the vibrations of others who have prayed there, cried there, or sought God there. When the sense of touch is not fully developed, not only are we capable of being abusive, but we tend to grab onto things or people—we want to possess them, as if somehow the answer to our longing were contained in the object or person.

With age, the skin receptors become less sensitive and we may be less capable of accurately feeling physical textures. But while our elders may have callused hands and worn touch receptors, it is still important that the quality of the touch we provide remains true and honest. A gentle pat on the shoulder is an easy way to help make a person feel appreciated and recognized. I've often observed participants, on their way to their seats, touching the people they pass in a kind of a wordless greeting. And I've seen the smiles and softening of the faces of those on the receiving end.

When I ask people what brings them joy, a recurring theme is how much comfort the physical presence of their pets brings them. Danielle often talks about how much she loves her dog, Fluffy. "He comes running when he sees me," she'll say. "I hold him on my lap and we cuddle. The touch of his soft fur makes me feel so good."

Over the course of her life, my mother underwent six major cancer surgeries. At the time of one of the earlier ones, when I was still a toddler and the technology was less advanced than it is today, the nurses had difficulty bringing her back to consciousness. She was a small woman and they weren't as aware in those days of the relationship between anesthesia dosage and size. In the recovery room, the nurses had trouble awakening her. They kept saying, loudly, "Mrs. Sabersky! Mrs. Sabersky!" When this wasn't working, they started shouting her first name: "Bettina! Bettina!" Still no response. Later, she told me, "I could hear them, but I couldn't move a muscle. I couldn't do a thing. Then, one of the nurses took some Vaseline and touched it to my lips. And that brought me back." It was almost as if she was saying, that touch saved my life. And then she said, "No gloves. Just the gentle touch of a finger on my lips." When you're vulnerable, everything is magnified, both negatively and positively. In my mother's situation, she felt that this human touch brought her back to life.

The Elderwise Way: No matter where we are in the evolution of our own sense of touch—from grabby and holding on, to deep respect for all people and all things—we can continue to grow throughout our lifetime by cultivating this sense. We support an elder's sense of touch by modeling warmth and acceptance: shaking hands with one another or giving a gentle hug and, as well, by acknowledging and respecting the space between one's self and another. Handling and examining objects from nature, like pinecones, rocks, crystals, or flowers, also supports this sense. Some people especially enjoy working with clay in the summer. They find pleasure in the cool, damp feel of this earthy material that changes its shape according to their touch, and results, ultimately, in a tangible piece to hold and bring home. With each tactile experience comes connection.

Sense of life

After we realize we are separate from our mothers and have become aware of the boundaries of our bodies through the sense of touch, we move on to understanding the inner workings of those bodies through the sense of life. This sense informs how we feel:

- Do I feel well, less well—or downright rotten?

- Do I feel healthy and strong, or do I feel tired and ill?

- Am I comfortable, or do I have a feeling of discomfort or pain?

- How's my energy?

The way for us all to learn this sense is to have direct experience of our own limits. Am I hungry? How hungry? Can I wait before eating? Can I focus on something other than my hunger while I wait? Am I tired? Am I so tired I need to rest or can I walk further? Am I thirsty? Do I need to use the restroom? In other words: What are my limits, and can I put up with a bit of discomfort?

Imagine addressing one's self with the following inner monologue: Does my body feel burdened with achy knees, upset bowels, or organs not operating properly? Am I going to succumb to these pains and complain—what some have called the "organ recital"? Or, can I somehow create a bit of distance from my afflictions? Can I separate my weak or painful body from my feelings or moods? I may be dependent on my senses, but, using my mind, I can, to some extent, control those senses (not talking about severe pain) and learn to choose how I think and feel and respond to my discomfort. Wait a minute here, I get to decide!

With age, we experience a weakening of our life forces—there is less energy and less vigor. But along the way we develop inner strength—the ability, to one degree or another, to choose how we think and feel and respond to our physical being, to be aware of our bodies but not completely directed by their demands and limitations. How can one get from the "organ recital," the feeling that *I am my pain*, to an increasing level of freedom? How can one calm and quiet the inner complaints of the body so as to focus on something else?

Thinking of others—that's the magic pill. Focusing on another helps take us beyond our awareness of our own issues. When compassion takes over, the focus shifts away from ourselves and our problems. To do for others has this wonderful side benefit and we can support our elders by encouraging them to do what they can for others in their lives.

Making soup for a sick friend, writing a get well card, smiling and being friendly, prayer, even just thinking about another—all are ways of taking action that give us a feeling of meaning and purpose. Thinking of others is the best cure for preoccupation with the body.

The Elderwise Way. While frail elders may not be able to help others in familiar ways, we can guide them toward other, possibly new, modes in which they can give or share. A lot of older people feel that they don't have anything to give to others—they can't even take care of themselves. This is especially true of people with memory loss. But every relationship is reciprocal and we can remind people that they are still responsible for their side. How they treat other people makes a difference. A smile or a laugh or a kind word, given or received, can help a frail elder understand that they still have a lot to contribute.

Helping a frail elder feel a sense of belonging to a community, one in which they have something valuable to offer to the group as a whole, supports the sense of life for both the elder and for the community. When you're part of a community, you understand that you have a responsibility to that community, and that your presence—and your behavior—matters.

Movement and Balance

The sense of movement works very closely with the sense of balance. Together, they allow us to operate in relation to the world while keeping our equilibrium. Gaining control over our body is an important developmental accomplishment, though we all, of course, achieve a different level of mastery over our kinesthetic movements depending on our innate abilities, desires and efforts—from standing on our own two feet to gymnastic feats.

A child learns how to stand and walk at around the same time that they learn to speak. Achieving these extremely significant accomplishments simultaneously is doubly empowering. No wonder we have the "terrible twos," drunk with these two commanding senses. *I am standing up, I can speak—look at me: I am here!*

After learning to walk, we get pretty good at balancing and soon start to trust that we won't fall. Balance uses receptors of the inner ear to give us the ability to maintain an upright posture; it gives us a reference point for relating to the rest of the world and allows us to move without losing our stability. We can walk around without even thinking about our balance! It is then that we start to take that sense of balance for granted.

On the other end of the spectrum, when elders lose the ability to stand or speak, or both, these dramatic losses threaten our sense of self. For those who have spent the first seventy or eighty years of their lives strongly identified with the upright posture and verbal ability to communicate this can be devastating.

I remember climbing down an icy mountain with my husband a very long time ago. He did it effortlessly, but I teetered along, imagining that the next step could send me sliding down the icy slope to my death. It took me a very long time to get down! The experience left me with a visceral memory of how it feels not to trust my balance in the world. It has given me a better understanding of what it might be like sometime in the future.

Will a person's psychological well-being deteriorate along with a decline in quality of movement, ability to walk, or ability to keep one's balance? This depends on the individual's capacity to transform their declining outer feeling of freedom and autonomy to an interior feeling of independence and self-sufficiency.

With age, none of us can move the way we used to. I can't run or jump the way I once did, but I still can get pleasure from the movements that I am able to do. And I do my best to take pleasure in—rather than feeling envious of—the movement of others who can do the things I could in the past. Today, I was talking with a young man who works at Trader Joe's. He was telling me how he gets up early for work and spends his afternoons at the beach. It's not that I don't still love spending an afternoon at the beach, but it's no longer what I want to do every day. It's not just my abilities that change, but my desires as well. Some things we outgrow.

As we age, our goal in relation to balance is to achieve an internal equilibrium, a deep calm, a place in which we can naturally balance giving and receiving, thinking of others as well as ourselves. In this place of calm, we don't have many needs. So many times I have heard from the elders around the table that they don't need anything—that the material world doesn't really "have anything" for them anymore.

Yet the need to give and receive is still there, just not so much on the material level—as long as one's basic needs are met. We all seek connectedness, community, and love. Whether we are old or young, we can give the meaningful gift of time, especially if another is lonely; we can notice sadness in another, listen, and offer encouragement. It doesn't take much to give a smile to a lonely person, to share a laugh in the checkout line, or to show those you love that you care.

The Elderwise Way. We know that, regardless of one's movement abilities, it is important to exercise and move regularly throughout the day. What we aim for in relation to the sense of movement is that—even with those movement-related losses that occur with age, injury, or disease—we can still access the inner feeling of independence that we had when first standing up and gaining control over our bodies.

We do our best to enable participants to
be as physically balanced as possible,
while seeking equilibrium
at a deeper level.

We also know that physical balance and balance-related reflexes decline with aging or disease. Taking advantage of the close relationship between movement and balance, we focus on both during our Elderwise exercise sessions, thereby maximizing the benefits of physical movement, body centeredness, and spatial awareness. We do our best to enable participants to be as physically balanced as possible, while seeking equilibrium at a deeper level. And we strive to help them recognize and appreciate the differences between inner and outer balance. Despite any further losses of physical balance, our goal is to be able to continue to give with self-assurance and without reservation. We can reach out and give with our hands, arms, and heart. We can also receive in a similar manner as we develop and increase our understanding of this process of giving and receiving.

We enjoy movement that is adjusted to our collective abilities, and we each present our self from the reference point of where we currently stand. As we move and sing or speak or reach out away from our center to challenge our balance, we can expand ourselves and fill the entire room with our essence. We move to music that awakens our joy in physical activity, we move in a social or coordinated way with others, and we use our imaginations to move us beyond the limits of our material bodies. Through imagination, the small movements of which one is capable—and the enjoyment of such movements—can provide a feeling of spaciousness.

We integrate activities that support the sense of balance by enhancing awareness of the space around us, including the front-to-back space, the side-to-side space, and the above-to-below space. We shift our weight, we reach away from our core, we adjust our balance while sitting or standing.

In addition, we take advantage of the close relationship of balance to movement, hearing, and speech. Songs, sounds and words go well with different movement patterns. We work to incorporate all of these sensory modalities into an exercise program for balance enhancement. And, ultimately, balance is nourished by opportunities for giving and receiving.

A CONFUSION OF DIRECTIONS

by *David Leek*

There is a barely noticed intention
That drives me in a confusion of directions.
It awakens me to many possibilities,
But, leaves me confused by the choices I must make.

I have learned from the past to predict my future.
But, I am slow to accept that this present moment
Is disappearing, second by second,
Like a droplet on a leaf, under a bright sun.

Just so, do my predictions crumble
In the dry heat of unfolding experience.
In an unending wave
That sweeps through my hopes and assumptions
Carrying me far past my narrow expectations.

I am very slow to learn acceptance
From this mix of hope and longing.
It is always my last choice,
Put off by my stubborn wish
To be in control of myself, and my life.

But, if I pay attention,
It's possible that I will fall backwards
Into understanding, step by step.
Like a lost detective
Meeting himself in a mirror.

CHAPTER NINE:

The Four Feeling or Emotional Senses

Personal engagement with each other.

As we engage with the world, we awaken to a complex interweaving of our sensory experiences and our internal responses to the things to which we are exposed.

The feeling senses—smell, taste, vision, and warmth (temperature)—inform our emotions. They take us beyond the experience of our physical body—a closed system—and help us to expand our relationship with the world. Through the feeling senses, we interact and exchange energy with our environment. We breathe in and are enveloped by smells from the outside; we ingest and taste food; we visually perceive objects and activity within our environment; we take in heat from the sun and radiate warmth from our bodies. These feeling senses allow us to fully interact with the world, whether we're appreciating beauty or are appalled by ugliness, whether we're licking our lips with delight or curling them in disgust. We are stirred by odors foul or sweet; we can get heated up with emotions, or feel cold and closed off from others and even ourselves. As we engage with the world, we awaken to a complex interweaving of our sensory experiences and our internal responses to the things to which we are exposed.

Smell

Smell is a prime example of the senses through which we interact with the world. We constantly "breathe in," exchanging oxygen, carbon dioxide, and other gases with the world around us. With good smells, we breathe in deeply and experience joy and relaxation. Breathing itself is relaxing to the nervous system. A bath with lovely smelling soap, a walk in the forest, a loaf of freshly baked bread, a baby, a lover: we breathe in deeply and feel that it is "good."

On the other hand, we can step in dog feces—my pet peeve—or come across a Porta-Potty, another's bad breath or unhygienic clothing, and feel that it is "bad." We make judgments. We may take shallow breaths, or even hold our breath for short periods, when we don't want to let that unpleasant smell in. Smell is a sense that we cannot block out: we cannot decide *not* to breathe, so we are ultimately forced to smell.

It is also true that this is the sense to which we become most quickly acclimated, but even if the odor doesn't linger with us for too long, when we smell something, we usually have an opinion about it. To varying degrees, we think, *This smells good* or *This smells bad.* Our "sensory opinion" may inform our reasons for getting close to others, or for keeping our distance. Smell is a very intimate sense: we may feel that we can smell the essence of another's being.

Another aspect of the sense of smell is its relation to the breath. If anyone asked me the two most important exercises, I would say, "Deep breathing and ankle pumps." Both help with balance and circulation. If you breathe deeply and rhythmically for even a few minutes, your system will appreciate it, not just your physical body but your emotional body as well. Aside from the sense of smell itself, the pure act of breathing is so beneficial. Many of us are shallow breathers. It's a reflection of the stress and anxiety in our lives, and the speed at which we go through our days. It can help us to slow down and take a deep breath.

The Elderwise Way. We support the sense of smell in order to encourage each of us to be less judgmental, and more open and welcoming to all. We do so through such activities as baking aromatic food, adding fragrant herbs to the soup cooking on the stovetop, using lavender soap, and burning beeswax candles. Everyone within that enhanced olfactory environment benefits. We model a welcoming setting for new and old participants and visitors; the smell of bread in the toaster, fresh coffee, fresh flowers, and pine branches are some ways to say, *This is a good place and all is well.*

Taste

Taste is different from smell in that we have a choice about what we put in our mouths. We can choose to eat certain kinds of foods and not others. We can choose the rate at which we eat, the amount, and how often we eat. Throughout our lives, what we choose to take in, how carefully we taste, and the speed with which we eat changes. Norbert Glas, in *The Fulfillment of Old Age,* likens the sense of taste to the manager of a company who purchases, or takes in, what is needed and politely refuses what may be offered but not needed.[4]

With aging, there may be loss of taste for a variety of physiological reasons. Some meals are enjoyed more than others. Rather than complain about the food, with maturity we take in what we like and, as in the company analogy, politely refuse what we do not need or what does not agree with us.

The Elderwise Way. Expanding and deepening the definition of what we mean by taste, our goal is to support the continuing development of tact and

---

4   Norbert Glas, *The Fulfillment of Old Age,* 103

courtesy, so that we all do our best to never knowingly insult or treat anyone in an offensive manner. When something is done in this way, we say it is tastefully done. We support this goal by modeling tactfulness and politeness, by sharing a blessing and a meal at the table, by trying new foods offered by others, or by respectfully declining.

Vision

The eye is an amazing organ of accommodation and adaptation. The eye's retina receives images that are upside-down and backwards, and then turned right-side up again in the brain. It accommodates to objects of different sizes seen from different distances, adjusting the lens as needed.

There is a visual exercise in which you can stare at something red and then stare at a white wall and you will see red's complementary color—green. Just now, I was staring out the window and then looked at a white wall and saw the window's shape on the wall. The eyes and their underlying neurophysiology have a great ability to adapt and, seemingly, this sense is always seeking balance.

With aging, we often have visual deterioration, even major loss or blindness. Nonetheless, the *sense* of vision is still there: you may just see things differently. My mother, who in her 90s had glaucoma and significantly impaired vision, still had her favorite oak trees that she enjoyed on her daily walk. Whenever she approached them, she would stop and say, "I don't just see my oak trees, I see the Lord in the oak tree." Beyond the limitations of her two eyes, she developed a highly sensitive kind of vision that you could call a third eye, *the third eye of wisdom.* The physical eyes may let you down, but the eye of wisdom always retains the potential for you to see more deeply.

The Elderwise Way. Taking the lead of the eye and its constant efforts to adapt to what it perceives, we encourage deeper development of each individual's inner peace and harmony. This is not to say that the "eye" cannot be critical and judgmental, finding flaws or imperfection. We even have the concept of *a critical eye*. Our hope is to encourage the expansive eye as opposed to the critical, judgmental eye.

We help support this expansiveness in advancing age by offering opportunities for appreciating beauty—beauty found in the natural world, as well as the beauty of artwork, our own and that of others. The study of composition, color, and the miracle embodied by a flower, or even an image of a flower, can awaken one's appreciation of the beauty around us. George mentioned that after painting flowers at Elderwise, he found himself looking more closely at the flowers in his garden at home. "There is so much more to look at in each one," he said. "I had no idea."

We set the table with care, paying attention to the nametags, the arrangement of coffee cups, and especially the centerpiece. In the center of the table, there is always something from nature arranged on colorful fabric in a thoughtful manner. At one point, we even had a staff position titled Director of Beauty!

Temperature

Our sense of temperature changes with external conditions, such as the heat of the sun or the setting of the thermostat. It also responds to inward, bodily conditions, such as movement-induced heat, the intake of food and drink, and one's emotional state. (Sometimes I think something negative and my whole body responds: *I shouldn't have done that*, I silently tell myself, and I am instantly hot and flushed.)

The job of the circulatory system is to adjust our inner thermostat. With normal aging, there is less flexibility in the circulatory system's ability to adapt to changing temperatures. This makes us more dependent on external heating and cooling, and we pay more attention to layers of clothing to keep our temperature balanced.

With the warmth and coolness of the sense of temperature, we are talking about more than just body temperature. We are also concerned with what you could call inner or "heart temperature"—the warmth of caring and empathy for others. With aging, we can be at risk for not just a cooling of our bodies, but a cooling of our feelings also, if the inner heart temperature has cooled too much. I've seen occasions of an older person's partner passing away, and it's as if they hardly notice it, so disconnected have they become from the warmth of their hearts. *Well, I guess I better get my hair done.*

Or, on the contrary, we can become heated with frustration brewing just below the surface. Norbert Glas[5] talks about the excessive internal heat that can build up in a person and, without an outlet for activity in the outer world, this heat keeps accumulating, creating irritability and the need for fresh air. I've worked with people who have to have the window open, they always have to have air moving, they are frequently red in the face. Sylvia, living with Parkinson's disease, which progressively made movement on her own more difficult, carried an almost constant sense of frustration that bubbled beneath the surface. Her frustration came out as anger and impatience with others. She was often overheated and red-faced. She couldn't express what she wanted to say, she couldn't move the way she wanted to, and she was confused. Painting at Elderwise was a wonderful outlet for her. Once, I asked her what she liked about it and she said, "I can do it myself."

The goal derived from the sense of temperature is to maintain the warmth of feeling for others—despite hardened arteries and cooling of the body that may call for more external heat and additional clothing—and to continue to have meaningful engagement and outlets with the world so as to dissipate excess heat. By doing both, we keep our inner and outer temperature balanced.

The Elderwise Way: We aim to make sure everyone is physically comfortable temperature-wise by attending to and adjusting clothing layers, ambient heat, window position, and water intake. Danny likes to keep his coat on for a while, sometimes because there is a chill in the room, and sometimes it just takes him a few minutes for his inner temperature to adjust to being with others. We stimulate inner warmth when people feel welcomed to the Elderwise community. *"I am interested in this group and it is here for me—there*

---

5 Norbert Glas, *The Fulfillment of Old Age,* 49

is a seat at the table with my name there. I am expected and welcome here." We aim to please—some like hot tea and others cold water. We want your cup to be filled with what you desire.

Over the course of the day, we stimulate warmth by taking in the natural beauty around us; by singing and telling stories; modeling a strong caring for each other through deep listening, writing cards for our friends that are ill, and honoring the passing of those that we have known in the program.

Working with paint, clay or other artistic mediums can give one the time to get in touch with one's self and satisfy the need to create. Being part of meaningful conversation where the time is taken to listen and understand each person can also be beneficial in ridding one of excess heat and creating more peace.

With maturity, just as the body patiently distributes the heat in order to gain temperature equilibrium, we also can strive for balance and develop patience towards others and ourselves. We can embrace acceptance, gratitude, and forgiveness. We can show our interest in, love for, and devotion to others. And we can strive to maintain warmth—both inside and out.

LISTENING

by *David Leek*

Listening is most interesting
When sound is soft
And feeling is tender.

Shouted words and bombastic language
Raise our protective shields
And draw us into rigidity.
Even worse, they trigger animosity
And tempt us then, to return the fire
Of anger, insult and refusal.

Tenderness is undefended.
It is open and hopeful.
Tenderness invites connection
By offering empathy, interest and respect.

Tenderness defuses anger
By opening the heart
To the underlying pain
That rage denies and conceals.

Anger offers us the hope of victory over another,
So that few may dream of vanquishing
What we fear, or do not understand.

But, beneath anger is impotence;
The terrible inability to change
What we fear in ourselves,
And others.

Listening comes with maturity,
It brings the understanding
That each of us stands separate,
And each of us longs to believe
That our views, our values, our solutions
Are true and deserve concession, understanding,
Respect and warm consideration.

It is so easy to forget
That we have these gifts to offer to others
In each and every moment,
In each and every connection
With each and every being we meet.

CHAPTER TEN:

The Four Spiritual Senses

Engaged in active listening.

The heart of the spiritual senses—hearing, speech, thought, and ego—is manifested as *an increasing inner quiet*. Ram Dass says this very simply and very well: "The quieter you become, the more you can hear." This does not refer only to external sound. The quieter and calmer and more peaceful the mind, the more we can understand our true nature. Each of the four spiritual senses gets progressively quieter. If you're talking, you can't listen; if you're making noise, you can't hear what's going on around you; if your mind centers on your personal needs (*I need to do this, I need to do that, I have to take care of this or that*), then it's hard to let in the needs of another.

As we hone our awareness of these spiritual senses, our self-involved ego becomes quieter and we become increasingly able to be present with another's experience.

Hearing

When we hear the sound of pottery being tapped, or the singing of a wet finger along the rim of a crystal glass, we can hear right into the heart of its origin. With aging, the amount of auditory information we are able to take in may diminish, but we can still have the experience of listening deeply. We can thus appreciate the simple sounds of nature, the sound of a loved one's voice, a beloved piece of music. Sometimes hearing one resonating note can be fully satisfying.

While we can learn an enormous amount by listening to the sound of another's voice, we often fail to really hear because we are not silent enough within. On the other hand, some of us are quite attuned. I used to hate to call my mother whenever I was upset, or even tired. All I'd have to say was, "Hi, Mom!" in what I thought was a bright and cheerful voice, and she would instantaneously respond, "Is everything all right?"

On the other end of the scale, we have one Elderwise participant who, whenever it gets quiet, almost immediately says, "Ho-hum," as if to say, "Let's get on with things!" There is clearly not enough noise for her, a reflection of her need for outside stimulus, something to fill in the spaces inside her mind. When people are uncomfortable with silence, it frequently is a reflection of their discomfort with their own challenging thoughts.

The Elderwise Way: We strive to create an environment that supports participants becoming more comfortable with quiet and more aware of the quality of the sounds they are hearing. We use ceramic mugs and real glasses rather than plastic ones when possible, in part because there's an alive quality to the sound of china on wood or the clinking of a glass. Listening to music—especially live music—is another wonderful way to open ourselves to the subtlety and layers contained in even the simplest sound. Once we had a musician visitor to Elderwise who played his upright bass for our group. The sounds were so low and deep, I can still feel them resonating inside my mind and being.

To further support the participants' comfort with inner and outer quiet, we incorporate deep listening into the conclusion of our exercise time. We take a moment to sit silently, aware of our bodies, tuning into the circulation and the breath that are now flowing freely after movement. We focus on our own feeling of well-being, and then, because we have created that space within ourselves, we make an effort to send that feeling to others who may be in similar situations. Moments like this support our ability to think of ourselves and others more compassionately, as well as our comfort with outer and inner quiet.

Speech

Speech is powerful. It comes from deep within us: *I believe this,* we say, *I think that. This is my opinion.* The sense of speech concerns both the *understanding* and the *power* of the spoken word[6] whether we are listening to another or speaking ourselves. In Hinduism, the presiding deity of speech is Agni, the god of fire, reflecting the power of the word and the courage required to speak.

It requires a certain amount of inner quiet in order to even know what we want to say. With aging and maturity, we hope we've gained some control over both our inner landscape and the words that come out of our mouths. Ideally, we don't want to hurt anyone with our words, we want to use them wisely. This can be particularly challenging within families, and the addition of dementia into the family dynamic often brings the stresses to the surface in not very pleasant ways. We snap, "I've heard that story a million times," or "You already told me that," or just avoid seeing that person because it's too painful or irritating.

---

6 Norbert Glas, *The Fulfillment of Old Age,* 119

Because it's challenging, we often don't give people with memory loss the opportunity to express themselves, and the time and the help they need to formulate and get out their thoughts. That's why we call our discussion group *supported discussion*—the support is the cane that allows them to access their thoughts and opinions, and express them.

The Elderwise Way. We make space daily for individuals to speak. We cultivate the habits of listening, speaking, and sharing one's thoughts. We support an elder's sense of speech by reading or reciting poetry aloud, singing, engaging in expressive movement, and by providing opportunities to speak. We encourage listening deeply to others, even if they have difficulty expressing what they want to communicate. Painting is a valuable way to foster expression, but to be able to express in words, and be understood, and be part of a big important conversation, is powerful. And that's how they leave at the end of the day: feeling valued and empowered.

A new participant in the program, Henry frequently didn't really understand the conversation. But the new experience of painting gave him great pleasure, and when it was his turn to contribute to the discussion, he went off topic and talked about the paintings on the wall. Waving his hand energetically, he exclaimed, "Look how they are all there on the wall. They're all different and all there and all enjoyable to look at." Because we make a point to listen to everyone, the group is trained to make a space for each person to speak. So the group made such a space for Henry, and even though the general discussion had nothing to do with painting, everyone understood that it was important for him to express himself and make a contribution. We didn't just tolerate him, we were all there with him, and appreciated his calling our attention to the paintings: he opened our eyes, once again, to their beauty.

Thought

What is the difference between speech and thought? While there is obvious overlap in these processes, *thought* is the intellectual sense, it embraces the ability to grasp inherent connections as words flow one to another—that is, the ability to understand ideas—whereas *speech* is the bringing of those ideas into communication with others. With speech, you have something to say and you say it. With thought, you are following a string of ideas, either your own or someone else's.

We stimulate the intellect by encouraging people to follow a string of thoughts and, as facilitators, an important piece of our work is to listen extremely carefully, so that we can catch the gems that bring real life and meaning to our discussion. You might think it's odd to discuss intellect when you're working with people with dementia, but it's not. While we do simplify, we don't dumb down the intellectual conversation. We draw people into the train of thought by saying the same thing in lots of different ways—it's a creative process. In a guided discussion like this, we can frequently get to the same level of conversation that you can have at a dinner party with your peers. You just have to start really slowly, listen very carefully, and be patient with the process. You'll be amazed at what you will hear!

Even people who are well into memory loss can track complex ideas—if you keep the story alive. One way to do this is to have a theme for the day. The topic will be alive if it's real for the facilitators. I recall a time when our theme was seeds: from this tiny thing something giant can grow. That spring, I had been doing a lot of planting, so this was an idea that was alive in me.

In the morning, we had a packet of cosmos seeds, which we planted in some pots we had waiting on the table. The morning conversation was more chitchat; we talked about how amazing it is that seeds can grow and become a flower. We talked about people's gardens and what they liked to grow—all very concrete. We carried the theme of growth into our exercise period, imagining ourselves planting our feet in the earth, pushing up against the dirt to make our way out to the light and air and rain necessary for our growth, blowing in the wind, reaching towards the sun. When we got to discussion group in the afternoon, we looked at plants that had moved past the seed stage, marveling at the life that comes from a tiny seed. By that time, all I really needed to say to spark deeper discussion was, "Is there anything anyone wants to say about seeds?" The picture had been developed with the group, little by little, before I turned to them with that question. People chimed in with thoughts about soil and water and all the conditions conducive to growth, and how some seeds make it despite difficult conditions. Some trees are crooked because they grew up in a windstorm or a drought.

Roberta made the jump to a more universal application of the themes we were discussing. "Some seeds make it and other seeds don't. It's like children," she said. "Some of them also struggle because they have to grow up in difficult situations." She paused, then went on. "We should be more understanding of people, and what challenges they may have had in their lives."

Sometimes you can feel the effort that it takes to get out a thought. When Joe was new to the group, I remember his posture changing as he listened to our first discussion. He went from relaxing in his seat to an erect and forward-leaning position. When was the last time he participated in an intelligent discussion? I wondered. That day, we were talking about mood, starting simply: *If we looked it up in the dictionary or on Google, what would we learn there?* The conversation brought him forward one step at a time. First, simple questions like, *What is mood?* Later, more complex questions: *What is it like when you're in a good mood? What is it like to be in a bad mood? There are some people who are generally cheerful. Are you that generally cheerful guy, or are you that crotchety guy?* These may seem like really simple questions, but what may seem like too simple a question is actually a foundation for a more complex discussion. Even to say, *Are you generally cheerful?* or, *Are you crotchety?* gives an opportunity for reflection and insight, a space to share abstractly and, eventually, more personally. Joe had an opportunity to weigh in at each of these different steps, feeling his way toward the right words.

The Elderwise Way: The goal derived from the sense of thought is to achieve an even greater inner quiet and focus, so as to understand a string of words and their intended meaning. I have found that in the setting of dementia, despite an obvious slowing of cognitive pace or diminished language, with support—such as repetition, rewording, and simplification—people can still retain the ability to understand the concept being conveyed, as well as the capacity to get to the essence of the matter. By speaking carefully, framing and reframing the question, and by listening equally carefully to what a participant is trying to say, we can piece together a wonderfully enriching and meaningful discussion.

I have found that in the setting of dementia, despite an obvious slowing of cognitive pace or diminished language, with support—such as repetition, rewording, and simplification—people can still retain the ability to understand the concept being conveyed, as well as the capacity to get to the essence of the matter.

Ralph knows what he wants to say, but the words that come out don't make any sense. We are called upon to listen deeply, not just to the words he is saying but also to interpreting the gestures of his hands, the tone of his voice and the expression on his face. We know some of his personal history, which also helps us fill in some of the gaps in his speech. By listening with our eyes and our ears and our previous knowledge, we are often able to understand at least part of what he's trying to say. It is not that it is easy either for Ralph or for the rest of us—it can be very tiring—but it is an extremely satisfying and worthwhile experience, both for the one struggling to be understood and the one making the effort to hear more deeply.

We can all give somebody the opportunity to be a philosopher. One of my favorite things is to give people a chance to share their wisdom. I just shake my head in delight and wonderment at the depth of the conversation that's possible when you're sitting around the table with people with significant memory loss.

Just as a bee zeroes in on a flower, at Elderwise, I get to watch participants zero in on a thought and its expression. I can see the release and the joy when it happens: *I've spoken, and I've been listened to. I've been understood, and I've been part of a meaningful discussion.*

Ego

The ego means "I": *I* do this, *I* do that. It is *me* that acts in this world. It is also the last of the twelve senses and the most difficult sense to tame. Because we so identify it with our deepest self, we often get it confused with the essence of ourselves. We think that's who we really are.

The ego does not want to be quieted; rather, it wants to be totally in charge. It is true that we can't do without our egos in our day-to-day lives. It's what pays the bills and drives the car. But an excess of ego inhibits our mental well-being. It's like eating: you have to eat to live, but to eat in excess is unhealthy. Just so with the ego: to feed it excessively allows it to convince us that it is all there is of our identity. When it is successful in doing this, our life experience is narrowed. An unquiet ego tries to makes the whole world exist just in relation to itself.

So the challenge is, to the extent we can, to quiet that sense of "I," that limiting sense of self. Quieting the ego encourages an expansion of our deeper self-awareness and a fuller ability to appreciate the depths of another's being. It allows us to walk in another's shoes. With the subduing of the ego, we can become so quiet inside that we can better understand and recognize the intrinsic worth of another person. With this subdued ego, one is able to welcome another with compassion and an open heart, and to feel more connected with all of life.

The Elderwise Way. Our entire program is designed to support this open-hearted compassion and awareness. The ultimate goal of working through the senses is to make some real personal progress in this fundamental area. All the other pieces come together at this crucial point. Through everything we do, we encourage all involved to think of others, even in the simplest and least obvious ways. When we hold hands and bless before a meal, or light a candle before painting, we are using ritual to remind us of our deeper connection. Even those moments of quiet we take after exercise are a time to feel the connections we share. The subjects we discuss offer opportunities to think deeply and compassionately. All these things elevate the ordinary and help us to be in touch with the depth of who we are as humans. They invite us to be sufficiently quiet inside so that imagining the *I* of another becomes possible.

Tools for transforming our lives

With the help of the mind, we use the twelve senses to *experience and understand* the world; as we work with them, they can become tools for transforming our lives.

This concept of *transformation* applies beautifully to our work with the frail elder whose physical senses and abilities are waning. We can use our imagination to experience with our minds what we can no longer do with our bodies. Right now, our group at Elderwise is intergenerational: we have a volunteer who is in her twenties; I'm in my sixties; the participants are in their eighties. One day, I asked the group, "You've lived long lives. What might you say to a younger person who is seeking your advice?" Sylvia said, "Do what you enjoy. I can't sing as well as I used to, but I still enjoy it and I can still remember most of the words. I know that I may not always be able to remember them, but I can now, and I still love to sing them. There are some things I can't do, but I enjoy doing what I can do." Listening to her, I could tell she had that inner feeling of joy.

Henry was unable, either physically or cognitively, to follow the group in exercise. One day, I looked over and saw his arm swaying slowly from side to side to the rhythm of the music. There was a smile of pleasure and satisfaction on his face that was a delight to see. I feel that way about walking: grateful that I can do it (especially when my hip isn't hurting), aware that I may not be able to do it forever. But that doesn't stop me from experiencing joy in the present. Movement is one way to reach and expand beyond the limitations of a shrinking or impaired physical body.

Although there are important early developmental periods for each of the twelve senses, we always have the opportunity to further develop and nurture these senses at any given point over the course of our lifespan, and to benefit from the growth opportunities this offers. It is this continuing growth and development that Elderwise is designed to enhance.

CHAPTER ELEVEN:

Dementia and Spirituality

At peace with one's self.

It is not easy to watch the light of intellectual acuity dim. It takes an adjustment on our part to alter our expectations and appreciate that another light can come on in those same eyes: the light of the heart that can shine more brightly and joyously.

If we define spiritual as getting closer to the deepest part of who we are, our essence, or as the process of feeling more and more connected to all that is—an understanding of the unity of existence—then there is no reason for that essential awareness to be diminished, even with a diagnosis of dementia. This was one of our theories when we began Elderwise, and the years have validated that hypothesis. I have witnessed people lose their cognitive abilities while, at the same time, opening their hearts and their spirits.

My thoughts on spirituality and dementia are based, in part, on my understanding of *koshas* in Hindu philosophy. *Kosha* is a Sanskrit word that translates as sheath, covering, or layer. For a visual sense of the *koshas*, one can imagine an onion with its skin, outer layers, and inner layers—overlays. Think of the innermost layer as deeper, nearer to our essence, and the outer sheaths as farther from our essence. As such, the outer sheaths are considered to be made up of gross matter (like the physical body)—as the sheaths get closer to the essence, the matter becomes finer and finer, and more and more subtle. The essence is not considered matter at all, but rather, pure consciousness.

The Elderwise Way. Our goal is to enrich and nourish all the layers or sheaths, from the gross to the subtle. We do so for self-nourishment and to more fully support those in our care, as well as their personal support teams. The work is a gift, not only to others with whom we come in contact, but to ourselves, as we all evolve in the great journey towards wholeness and spiritual well-being.

If spiritual is closer to one's essence— one's true self—then it readily follows that spirituality can and does coexist with dementia.

The growing sense of heart

If *spiritual* is closer to one's essence—one's true self—then it readily follows that spirituality can and does coexist with dementia. The deeper essence shines through the heart and, regardless of the presence of dementia, a person is able to continue to develop the heart-sense qualities of kindness, joy, and love. This has certainly been my experience sitting around the Elderwise table with people affected by dementia. There are those who would argue that point with me. I have heard people say, about a person in the later stages of dementia, "There is no one left inside. There's nobody home." But, in my opinion, while there's life in the body, that essence is never gone.

I would like to share some stories that support this concept of the growing sense of heart and continued sense of self, even in the presence of dementia. Even in memory loss, the sense of self remains strong. Even with extreme memory loss, people use the pronoun *I* to talk about themselves, a way of asserting their continued existence.

I am thinking again of Teresa, pioneering climber of poles for Seattle's utility company. What a light she was! Her essence always shone through. She understood that, despite her dementia diagnosis, she hadn't lost the essence of who she was. She knew she couldn't find the right words, she was aware that she had a lot of trouble remembering things. Her biggest challenge was when she knew what she wanted to say but just couldn't find the words to say it. But she honored her essence and knew that her humanity wasn't diminished by her diagnosis. Her sense of self was so strong. She had spent a lifetime standing up for truth, standing up for women and the oppressed and, even in her memory loss, she talked about social justice causes with that same passion, even if she didn't remember the details. And if she couldn't think of the words for what she wanted to say, she would start doing what she called (and Ella Fitzgerald did, too) *scat*: vocalizing nonsense syllables to convey her thoughts. She delighted in making those sounds, as she delighted in nature or her painting, or whatever else she was involved with in the moment. It was easy to share those moments with her in sincerity and with pleasure and, together, we laughed.

Even when quite far progressed, she shared with others the joy of creating sound, the joy of the beauty of nature, the joy of caring about social causes, and the beauty of the people in front of her. One could understand that expression in whatever way it came out—in the color and movement on her paintings, the sincerity of her voice in talking about social causes, the joy of made up sounds and music, or the shared smile.

At Elderwise, the level of love and caring for one another is apparent every day. It is especially confirming to witness the unfolding of the palpable change that occurs when a new participant joins the group. It's amazing to witness: you would think that they were trained to welcome the next person, it's so automatic when new people come. Recently, when a man and his wife visited, the regulars overflowed with warmth and inclusivity. Almost as a joke, I asked him, "Do you feel welcome?" "Oh yes!" he said. "I'll be back."

John wasn't here for a week and, upon his return, Edith exclaimed, over and over, "Oh John! It's so good to have you back! We missed you so much!" As it happened, I had also been away the week before, so after Edith said this for the fifteenth time, I said, teasingly, "You know, Edith, I wasn't here last week either. Did you miss me?" She was taken aback a little. "Well, you know," she said, "I have trouble remembering things." Then Lila spoke up protectively. "That's why we're in this group," she said, "because we can't remember things." "Yeah," I laughed, "but you remembered him!" It was a funny moment, but it demonstrated to me again that they share something unique with each other, and that they know, no matter how much they appreciate the staff (and they do), that we are not part of the core group whose members share something special.

John's daughter gave me some insight into what her father had been like as a parent and his post-dementia late-emerging warmth. "He was a good man, a good provider who worked hard," she said, "but a little bit distant, more focused on his work than his family. But now, with his memory loss, he's available in a different way to my children. They do little everyday things together. They sweep the floor and do art projects. There's lots of hugging and snuggling, lots of warm smiles and mutual appreciation. It is good for me to see this," she went on, "but I'm also a little sad that I didn't have as much access to that part of my dad." I'm not saying that a bad person becomes good or that every person with memory loss has a heart of gold, but there's a real possibility that the heart can show itself more fully as the cognitive abilities decline.

One day, the group was singing, *"Love is all there is,"* over and over. Suddenly, I looked over and Cleo was sobbing. Since she had only recently joined the group, I didn't know her that well. I did know her well enough to be aware of how low her cognitive abilities were: when I took her to the bathroom, she was unable to get herself onto the toilet, couldn't figure out whether her pants should be up or down, or what the paper is for.

Edith, who was sitting on the opposite side of the table, went and put her arms around her. Then I went over and said, "What's going on, Cleo?" Through her tears, she managed to say, "That's what I am." "What are you?" I pursued. "Love!" she cried. "That's what I am."

Spiritual progress

The brain is our tool in this life to gain knowledge—material, intellectual and spiritual. We use the brain to question, to search, to think rationally and creatively. The intact physiological abilities of the brain make possible focus, clear thinking, and the will to improve the way one lives in the world. The brain is the vehicle that allows the mind to work and, to the extent that the brain is damaged, the focus, clarity, and will to support further intellectual development are impaired. It follows then that, to the degree that our physical brains do not function well, we are not able to use this tool to further our personal growth and development.

On the other hand, forces of habit carry us forward and reflect how a person occupied their mind before the onset of dementia. If we spent a lot of time studying chemistry, our minds will be occupied with chemistry. If we spent time playing the piano, our minds will be thinking about compositions during the day and, perhaps, even during sleep. In this way, our minds are habituated. If one is in the habit of contemplation or sharing love or thinking about the meaning of life, our minds, even with dementia, can continue to carry us forward on this path.

At Elderwise, I have seen people with dementia who have spent a lifetime noticing when others need help, rouse themselves—as Edith did when Cleo was crying—when someone is in need and do their best to help them. I have seen people like Teresa, habituated to wanting justice in the world, and to the activism that makes justice possible, continue to be concerned about the state of the world. I have seen people habituated to making puns, and to making art. These themes are carried forward and remain forces in later life—energetic grooves that people fall back into regardless of the state of their brains.

With the onset of dementia, this habituation continues. In other words, although people with dementia have diminishing brain-based abilities to will themselves to deepen spiritual work, create new habits, or initiate new ways of being, they are carried forward, to a certain extent, by the energetic force of what they have done in the past. It is a bit like the merry-go-round in the playground; even after you hop off, it continues to turn for a while. In the same manner, if one has led a life of spiritual practice before dementia, there will be an energy that continues to carry one along in this way.

Regardless of someone's diminishing abilities to deepen practices, learn new skills or come up with new ideas, the person with dementia has not lost any spiritual ground that was previously gained; in the most fundamental way, they are not less than they were before. Clearly, they have lost brain function, they have lost the tool that is used by the mind to make progress, but they have not ultimately lost the mind, only its ability to express itself through the intact brain.[7] Any spiritual progress they may have made is never lost.[8]

For those whose lifetime focus was more material, when they are forced out of the familiar way of life by loss of physical or cognitive abilities, this new way of living can provide opportunities to deepen their spiritual and emotional connections to themselves and others, as we saw with the relationship between John and his grandchildren. Edges can soften, hearts can open, stereotypes and prejudices can fall away.

Our final new experience

At Elderwise, we hope that the participants' experiences will help them to become more open, more loving, more willing to try new things, more confident, more joyful, more broad-minded, more expansive. Because death and what comes after death are, by definition, new experiences, I think it will be easier for people who are comfortable being more open and more willing to try new things to approach these ultimate challenges. For when an individual becomes more trusting and confident in who they are and, by extension, more tolerant of others, it greatly increases the chances that such a person will be open to and welcoming of whatever experience may come.

The Elderwise program began with the hypothesis that it is possible for people with dementia to grow in these ways. In our more than two decades of practice, our experience has proven this to be true. How is it that our participants can learn to be more open, more loving, more joyful, and just plain happier? In the same way that a blind person may learn about the world through a more developed and heightened sense of touch, a person who has limited cognitive abilities has the potential for a more heightened sense of heart. In providing a warm and supportive environment that recognizes and fosters this possibility, we can support this expansion of heart.

---

7   See Chapter 4, *The Concept of Wholeness and the Frail Elder: Mind Does Not Equal Brain,* for a more detailed explanation of this differentiation.

8   Bhagavadad-Gita, Chapter 6

A person whose brain is not working well can make better use of this heightened sense of heart and, paradoxically, can grow in joy and love, because they are less distracted by outer cognitive layers and experiences. As the cognitive layers fade and there is less mental capacity for growth, our experience suggests that there is an opening—an opening through which the deeper heart-focus is more accessible.

CHAPTER TWELVE:

Caregiving

The Dementia Care Partner

In the best of all worlds, the continuum of care for a frail elder living with dementia embraces a team approach. A frail individual requires more than the usual amount of support; this means, on the flip side, that someone has to do more than the usual amount of giving. That person (or persons) is called the caregiver. More recently, the term *care partner* has come into use as a way of recognizing that there is still mutuality in the relationship, that there are gifts to receive on both sides. This book is intended for the caregivers, and care partners, of the world—both family members and professionals.

I have not been the full-time caregiver for a frail elder for an extended period of time—though I was grateful to be with my parents in the weeks and months before they died—so I have not personally experienced the exhaustion, nor can I truly know what carrying the full responsibility (including financial responsibility) for another person entails. I have, however, been a professional part-time caregiver at Elderwise for over two decades, and this opportunity has helped me to understand the ideas that I now share.

Each person has their own path of coming to caregiving. The Elderwise approach fosters a deepening awareness in the caregiver of their own essence and that of others. Three concepts, or practices, are central to supporting this personal growth.

1. Giving care as a spiritual practice

2. Learning to quiet oneself

3. Learning to adjust and enjoy the new and changing relationship

Giving care as a spiritual practice

One of the founding principles of Elderwise is working from one's own essence. In doing so, one is always in touch with their own deepest part: This centeredness guides every movement and action. Whether I am serving tea, helping someone in the restroom, or communicating with another staff member, I always have the potential to be working and moving from my own center, my own core. This simple act of awareness spiritualizes everything I do.

If, simultaneously, I am engaged in the practice of another founding principle of Elderwise—recognizing the essence of others—then I am serving the highest in another person as well. It really doesn't matter what I'm doing, it can be paper work, waiting for buses to pick up participants, facilitating an art class, or providing personal assistance. If I am doing this happily and serving the highest in another, then that spiritualizes my work.

One can achieve this in most forms of work but, when caring for others, spiritualizing the work can come more naturally because the focus of awareness is directly in you and in front of you: your essence and the essence of another. The Buddhists call this way of being fully aware *mindfulness*—being aware and present in the moment to the current experience, whatever it may be.

When working in this manner, one's actions will be in alignment with one's thoughts, values, beliefs, and one's own deepest truth. Work thus becomes a life-affirming way of being. This awareness makes for a positive and enriching experience in which one can practice and progress in one's own spiritual goals, while caring for another.

Learning to quiet one's self

To go from the speed of Western life to the patience and tranquility needed to be with someone experiencing cognitive impairment is quite a transition. It requires a lot of practice in self-quieting. It's the same change of focus that is required to be fully with a child. The really fascinating discovery, however, is that you don't need to do much to truly *be* with another. A few words or actions here or there can create an environment in which the unexpected can emerge.

Once, when my nephew was five, he played the game of imitating his mother, grabbing her purse, rushing from one end of the room to the other, pretending that he had many important things to do and that everyone must hurry up. *First we have to go here, and then we must rush there. No time to dawdle!*

In the years that began when my oldest child started kindergarten, my mornings were filled with stress and pressure. I would hurriedly get three children up, dressed, fed, in the car, and ready for the day. Like my nephew's game, I was running around the house, rushing everyone along. No time to dawdle indeed!

So when people say, "How can you work with this population?" I honestly answer, I like the slow pace, the quiet, the calm. When I'm out in the world, my ears hurt. They hurt from cars honking. They hurt from long meetings and the noise of the city. I want the quiet, I want the calm, I want the slowed down sense of time. When people talk about the program, they talk about that feeling of just being able to be and slow down and not be in what feels like the competitive, judgmental, rushed, never-enough state that we occupy much of the time. Elderwise is not like that, and it's rare.

One of the beautiful things that
can occur from within the act of
being quiet and creating this loving space
is that the person with dementia feels
an invitation to open up.

One of the beautiful things that can occur from within the act of being quiet and creating this loving space is that the person with dementia feels an invitation to open up. The wind has stopped blowing so hard, the sun is giving a little warmth, the muscles can relax. Everything is calm and open and safe. Who knows what opportunities for connecting and sharing, what words of wisdom and love, will come out when the environment is quiet?

We currently are working with a group comprised mostly of men. I sometimes see them out with their wives and they are mostly silent. Their wives are taking beautiful care of them, but there is a different dynamic when one is operating as part of a couple—especially one in which one member is functioning as caregiver—and when one is part of a group of one's peers. When the men come together around the table, we make sure that each individual is given the space to talk without feeling that there is a clock ticking away the time allotted to them before others grow impatient with their efforts. They all have trouble expressing themselves; they all have trouble finding thoughts or finding words. And they are so encouraging of one another as they work really hard to share what is meaningful and is longing to be expressed. One man recently talked about how delighted he is to be able to experience the camaraderie and loving support of this group who openly share common struggles.

Adjusting to the new relationship: Enjoying life in the present

To take the time to consciously enjoy the taste of an almond, the color of the sky, the feel of walking, and the heart-to-heart connections we make with others, allows those of us who work and live with persons with dementia a growth experience that enriches both the caregiver and the care receiver. The frail elder begs us to live in the present, to meet them where they are, and to focus our attention on what is here now. When we do, a moment of connection is created, one that invisibly but solidly weaves its way through the mundane and often challenging demands of living with one another.

> The frail elder begs us to live in the present, to meet them where they are, and to focus our attention on what is here now.

Over the years, I have noticed that since we did not know a person before they developed dementia, frequently it is easier for me and my colleagues to enjoy the relationship with someone with cognitive impairment than it is for family members. We relate to the person as they are now, with no set expectations connected to what came before, without the awareness of all that they have "lost."

And I'm constantly reminded that, despite the losses, not only does so much remain but the heart is perhaps more open to love and connection than it was before. There is joy in discovering the kinds of connections that you can have now; connections that can be very deep and very meaningful. Professional caregivers can help show family members—who may be devastated by the absence of "the person they once knew"—how to enjoy the changed relationship.

One spouse told me that her husband, "Goes to the club (that's what he calls Elderwise) four days a week. The other three, we pretend we're on a cruise." Taking advantage of what he likes to do, they go on long walks together, something they both enjoy. She has learned, like many other caregivers, that to catch what is in the present through keen observation is the new habit that care partners need to cultivate. Like many other caregivers, she has learned to discern and expand on the vitality in the present moment.

And, there is a pattern I sometimes see with family members that involves a "testing" of the person with dementia. *What did you have for breakfast? Who came to visit this weekend? What are the names of your children?* This is a form of laying a trap that family members (and professional staff as well) need to train themselves out of doing. Bringing attention to the gaps in memory helps no one.

While people with dementia will sometimes remember the "facts," and share something surprising with you, frequently those questions just make people feel worse about themselves and their situation. When this happens, you can soften certain blows. If someone can't remember his wife's name, don't focus on that. Instead, you can say, "I know how close you two are." You can even mention the forgotten name, without it being a correction. "I know," you might say, "how important Lily is to you." It doesn't mean she's less valuable because you can't remember what to call her. It doesn't mean you love someone less because you can't remember their name.

There are ways to elicit responses that don't have anything to do with the individual's recall abilities. Depending on the progression of one's cognitive impairment, one can still create, have ideas and opinions, share a laugh, and experience deep joy and connection. When family members learn to make this adjustment, everyone is typically much happier.

It is possible to learn not to ask what someone had for breakfast, or try to dig for any other unimportant piece of concrete information. Instead, we can make observations that allow the person to comment on something that has nothing to do with memory. Rather than proving what they don't know, we can create an atmosphere in which both parties can enjoy what they are experiencing as they more fully share the present moment.

You can even talk about complex ideas, about courage or what it means to be an elder. You can talk about how you each feel about death. You can talk about almost anything, including important ideas, while avoiding questions that challenge the memory and create anxiety in both the questioner and the one groping for an answer: *How many brothers did you have? Where did you grow up? What year were you born?* It may take a little while to make this shift, because, as a culture, we take for granted that it is these "facts" that demonstrate our identities.

I'll tell my mother-in-law, who has advanced dementia, "I like your new haircut," or, "I see you're dressed all in blue." This gives her an opportunity to respond in the moment. "Yes," she'll say. "Everything matches!" She'll gesture to the outside and I can't tell if she's gesturing to the sky or the buildings, the trees or the wind, but she is excited to share that moment with me and that is far more important than my understanding the specifics of what she's seeing. We both get joy out of cutting through the isolation in which so many of her moments are lived. There are days when I go visit her that I start out in a grumpy mood. Often I am surprised to realize how much happier I am after being with her. There is something about sharing that inarticulate love that is deeply uplifting and gratifying.

CHAPTER THIRTEEN:

Continuum of Care

There is that time in life when all of us may enjoy the coffee shop, tavern, book club, exercise class—opportunities to meet with friends or colleagues to socialize, accomplish a common purpose, and share our lives and our stories. At some point, though, whether it's because of decreased hearing or vision, desire for less stimulation, or a slowing of cognitive processing, less and less of the outer world can be comprehended. It is at this point that a person living with dementia may no longer be able to process and take in the whole group.

At Elderwise, we might notice that a participant is preoccupied with the crumbs on the table, or picking at their own clothing. Perhaps they will only talk to their neighbor—doing so regardless of what else is going on in the room—or need the constant attention of a facilitator. Even in our small group environment, we require that participants offer something to the group and are able to benefit from the experience of being there. There can be a high-energy cost to all when one person's needs repeatedly overwhelm those of the group. Some people can't say much, but they offer a warm feeling of love or joy. They may pat others on the back with a smile. That kind of open-heartedness will get you by for a long time.

But there's a certain point in the progression of the disease when a person can only attend to what is right in front of them. At this point, the rest of the group doesn't really exist for them. They are no longer able to go with the rhythm of the group; their own internal rhythm pushes out the awareness of others. Their anxieties and needs take over and require fulltime attention. Maybe they can see their neighbor, but that's it. The rest of the room is not present for them, and that means they're ready for a smaller situation. With Fred, it became clear that he was finding it more and more difficult to go with the flow. He became increasingly rigid and confrontational, unable to share. "This is my seat," he would say. "That's my yogurt container. That's my paintbrush. It's not yours. You can't use it. Give it back."

Harold was like Fred—very, very rigid. He had to hang his coat on *this* hook, sit in just *that* chair. If you go directly up against that kind of aggressive energy, it gets worse rather than better, so he took a lot of attention to manage. But he loved the group, so much so that even on weekends, when he had a caregiver, he would demand to be taken to Elderwise. "But they're not open," the caregiver would tell him. "Take me there," Harold would demand, and the caregiver would have to drive him all the way down to Elderwise to show him that the building was closed before he would believe him.

We worked with him and his family for many months, but it became increasingly clear to all of us that he was too disruptive. Our primary responsibility is to the group and its physical and psychic safety, so, difficult as it is to tell someone that they can't come anymore, we agreed that it was time for him to leave. Then, somehow, the transport bus didn't get the message that he was no longer attending our program. So, the next week, the bus went as usual to the adult family home where he lived and, being very mobile, he climbed on and rode it downtown to Elderwise. We used his unexpected appearance as an opportunity for him to say a final goodbye to his group of friends.

When we can see that somebody is getting closer to the point where they're not going to be able to stay in the program much longer, we do our best to talk to the family. We openly discuss the fact that it's getting harder for their loved one and that it is time to start thinking about the next step. And we always process the departure with the group after a participant has left. They, too, have been aware that it was getting too difficult for that person to be there. We always acknowledge, "So-and-so left because it was getting a little harder for them to be part of the group." They know that this was true. It is challenging for the group to have a member who increasingly doesn't function well in this environment, and it's also true that it is usually not the optimal situation for the participant either.

Physically smaller, but not spiritually smaller

At this point in elders' lives, their worlds may get physically smaller, but this doesn't mean that they have to get spiritually smaller. People naturally move from bigger groups to smaller groups and then, maybe, to just one companion at a time. Likewise, the quality of the environment frail elders choose may shift from louder to quieter, often with more quiet, alone time preferred. They often direct their attention to the smaller things—the flower arrangement, the tidied room, the view. Frail elders may get to the point where they are communicating on the cellular level: with sound, vibrations, scents, and loving thoughts. This progression underlies the concept of continuum of care, in which the supported opportunities we offer are constantly adjusting to match the social needs of the individual.

> At this point in elders' lives,
> their worlds may get physically smaller,
> but this doesn't mean that they
> have to get spiritually smaller.

I am not trying to say that declining is "no big deal," that it is not a problem, nor am I suggesting that dementia is not challenging and does not cause suffering. It does. Very significant losses occur. But if someone can no longer take in a broader experience, like the Elderwise group, that doesn't mean that a smaller, more optimal experience can't be provided to them. Still interesting and varied, still deep, just smaller. Until death, one does one's best to adjust the environment to make it best suited for the individual. The essence of everything is contained in the largest of the large, and the smallest of the small. It is as William Blake wrote in his poem:

> To see a World in a Grain of Sand
> And a Heaven in a Wild Flower,
> Hold Infinity in the palm of your hand
> And Eternity in an hour.

There is the same essence in a raindrop as in the downpour, the same essence in Blake's *Grain of Sand* as in the whole beach, the same essence in one musical note as in the whole orchestra. Each second contains eternity. So even if one is on one's deathbed with dementia, the soul has not changed. The loss—of the brain as a tool of learning and cognition—happened long ago. The brain and the physical body containing it will die, but the subtle mind is still there and will, in fact, be released from the dementia upon death.

NOT WRONG, NOT RIGHT

by *David Leek*

It is not for me to judge
If this moment be good or bad,
If this heartbeat be foolish or sad.

There is no right way; nor is there wrong.
Without intention, action follows impulse
Set free by hope, or ignorance,
Or the simple unwillingness
To sit still.

Waiting is mostly impatience;
But sitting still is an opportunity,
A ticket to plunge, without effort,
Into groundless being;
Not falling, nor flying,
But allowing all that is;
Recognizing it all without comparison,
Without boundaries, without preference.

It's like falling;
When everything seems to be moving while you are still.
Yet, you are sure to be awakened
When genuine stillness within
Opens you to life unlimited; open and free.

You don't need to dance
When dance is everything within you
And everything outside you is dancing
With you.

IN CONCLUSION

At Elderwise, our work-of-aging activities
support body, mind and spirit.
They include the physical and
the creative, the exercise and the art,
the meals partaken together
and the silences we share.

From the moment you walk into Elderwise, there is an environment of welcoming and acceptance. Time slows down to meet the speed of the participants. The setting, the practices, the attitudes, all are woven together to convey that each person—participant and facilitator alike—has a seat at the table, belongs in that seat, and has something to offer the group.

At Elderwise, our participants' work does not rely on memory or complex conceptualization. Instead, our work-of-aging activities support body, mind and spirit. They include the physical and the creative, the exercise and the art, the meals partaken together and the silences we share. They consist of in-the-moment contemplation and sharing of thoughts and experiences of such topics as forgiveness, courage, and recognition of a bumpy life journey.

We may have conversations around how we think about ourselves and how to deal with the down times. We talk about family, past work, what we value most, and the various kinds of legacy that we, as individuals, will leave. We don't shy away from discussing our mortality.

These conversations often flow from our reading or creating poetry, discussing proverbs, listening to or writing a group story with the help of a facilitator. Reflecting on music and how it makes us feel can also lead to deeper discussion, as can viewing and contemplating famous artworks—or even our own works of art, the creation of which expands each person's individual expression. These practices are woven into our programming for the frail elder.

In this manner, we offer opportunities to do the work of aging: to consider what it means to be an elder, and to take one's rightful place as a valued elder.

Almost all of the elders around the Elderwise table have been diagnosed with some kind of dementia. Yet, being there with us in the group setting, you might not be aware of each individual's cognitive impairment. I think of Margaret who, at 96, was very excited about each day. "I want to know what is coming next," she said. And I think of Betty. She was so content with her life, so full of gratitude for her family that she frequently broke out in old hymns or long ago memorized poetry. She had a great sense of humor and a lot of spunk. And she was ready to die. "I have no complaints," she frequently said. There have been many others like them.

There is, of course, sadness surrounding the diagnosis of Alzheimer's disease. Yet the compassion expressed by and felt from others can help to soften the impact of the difficult diagnosis. *Yes, we're in the same boat,* one participant might say; and another acknowledges that she can't find the words to express her thoughts. *You'll think of it later,* says yet another.

What you are most likely to see around the Elderwise table is life lived fully in the present and delight in the company of others: hilarious eruptions of laughter; honesty, reflection, tears, and compassion; and an understanding and acceptance of past challenges.

I have often overheard our day-program coordinator show our space to family members of potential participants and exclaim, "This is where the magic happens!" I am convinced of this. Each day, like a cafeteria or smorgasbord, Elderwise offers everyone at the table the opportunity to partake of some enriching and meaningful tidbits. Choice is always given: Take things that you enjoy; leave things that are too rich, too salty, or too bitter to digest at the moment.

Once, early on, when the Elderwise program was still in my home, I got stuck in traffic as I was headed back to meet a woman interested in working with me. When I arrived, full of apologies for being late, there she was, apron-clad, lighting a candle, interacting with the participants as if she had been there forever! The knowledge—the inspiration—was already within her. Within you, as well, lies the core of the Elderwise program: deep caring and respect for all human beings.

APPENDIX 1:

The Seeds for Elderwise

The seeds for Elderwise were planted when I was in my early twenties, working in my second job as a physical therapist in Southern California. But the soil in which those seeds germinated came from much earlier in my life. At fourteen, I became terrified of dying. Plagued by the profound questions of identity that teenagers often encounter—*What happens when you die? Are you suddenly nothing? How can I be nothing? How can I not be me?*—I would wake at night in a sweat of fear about existence and non-existence.

My parents were German Jews, people who fled the land of their birth to save their lives. My father was born in Berlin in 1920. It took his family so long to get out of Germany that, just a week after they left, their apartment was bombed. My mother was born in 1921. When she was fourteen, in 1935, her parents, while they tried to sell their family farm, sent her and her sister to Switzerland. When their parents finally escaped Germany, the family went to Cuba, one of the few places that would accept Jewish émigrés at that time. Mom studied piano in Cuba and learned Spanish, both of which enriched her later life. After a year, she left, ahead of her family, for California, where she had some other relatives. She took a boat, all by herself, to Miami. By the time I was born, she was married to my father and living in Pasadena, California, where he taught mechanical engineering at Caltech. He too had spent some time in Switzerland before coming straight to this country with his family. They chose to live in Los Angeles, so he could pursue his studies, and then his career, at Caltech.

When my older sister and I were children, my father seemed strict and impatient; not someone a child gravitates towards. He was better once we were grown up. I can still see him sitting next to me, helping me with my homework and thundering, *Think!* And then, a minute later, *Think!* Parents of that era could just look at you and you would quail. I don't know how they did that. You couldn't touch his shoes, spill your milk, be a kid. But he was a friend to those who struggled. He helped people through school. He cared about them as individuals, not just as students. He made a difference in people's lives, mostly by giving them extra attention, the extra push that helped them feel that they were valuable. There were always three or four students from the university at our home over holidays, kids who lived too far away to go home and who otherwise would have had their Thanksgiving or Christmas dinners in a cold dorm. It seemed normal to me to have these extra people at our table.

My home was very loving but also a little bit cold. We all pretty much lived in our rooms. Even though my mother and my sister were often there, I would come home from school to what felt like an empty house. Once, I sat in the little room off the living room (some people would call it a den, but that was too informal a word for my family) and read the newspaper. Coming out of her room, my sister discovered me there. "How bold of you!" she exclaimed. The only time we all got together informally was in the kitchen to have snacks. I suspect that it is this gathering around the kitchen table that is one of the origins of Elderwise.

I always adored my mother, but we didn't sit and talk. Among the things we didn't talk about were the six major surgeries for different cancers that she had when I was a little girl. In those days, this was not the sort of thing parents shared with children. I could tell, of course, that something was going on, something was wrong. Children always can. When I awoke fearful in the middle of the night I would call her to my room. "It's okay," she would tell me, with a deep assurance. "But how do you know it's okay?" I would demand. And she would say, emphatically, "I just know." I knew my mother didn't lie about other things, so that was going to have to be acceptable for the time being. But what did she mean by "okay"? And how could she be so sure? Even without knowing she had had cancer, it was clear that terrible things happened in the world. People got old and died. Was that okay too? So, without being aware that it was happening, my lifelong search began.

What I also didn't know was that Mom was a closet Vedantist, another thing not to be discussed in our conventional community. An ancient religion with origins in India, Vedanta affirms "the oneness of existence, the divinity of the soul, and the harmony of religions."[9] Strengthened by the belief that "even if we lose our body, our mind and soul live on,"[10] it is no wonder that she felt so deeply that, no matter what happened, it was, indeed, "Okay."

Mom came out of the spiritual closet in stages, and only to those closest to her. Most of her friends didn't know about her practice, didn't know that the characteristics that made her dear to them were the effects of that practice: her kindness and thoughtfulness, her generosity and genuine interest in others. Her soul mates were those who could understand the language of Vedanta. In her room, always, was a picture of her guru, Swami Prabhavananda, a kind-looking man with a beautiful countenance. If someone asked who he was, she would say, "A very dear friend." After my daughter died, she added a picture of Ramakrishna, a nineteenth century Indian mystic. That was coming more fully out of the closet.

It wasn't until I was a grown woman studying Eastern religion and philosophy that I began to understand why, in the midst of her own illnesses, she could reassure me with such conviction. In my teens, I had to keep functioning and keep going, so I pretty much stifled my quest. I was a soul spinning in space, knowing that there was some center in me, but not having either the tools or the language to discover where it lived and how to bring it into the light. But what I did have was time alone, time in which to think, time in which to be quiet and explore the silence.

It was only after I was in college that Mom took me with her to the Vedanta Center that she attended. Curious, and wanting to share the experience with her, I went a few times, but nothing happened. No lights went off inside me. I stopped going. It was many years later, after I moved to Seattle and

9 *What Is Vedanta?*, Vedanta Society of Southern California http://vedanta.org/vedanta-overview/ Accessed February 27, 2020.

10 Swami Bhaskarananda, *Death: A Transition*, Vedanta Society of Western Washington. http://www.vedanta-seattle.org/articles/death-a-transition/ Accessed February 27, 2020.

broke up with a boyfriend, that the search began in earnest again. I visited the local Vedanta Center and somehow knew I was home. There was someone there who could answer any spiritual question with an authority that comes from experiential knowing, someone who had only my best spiritual interest at heart, a monk, Swami Bhaskarananda. (He is now the senior-most monk of his order in this country.) Again, no lights went off, and I never analyzed the situation, I just never looked further after that. I had found a philosophy where someone knowledgeable could teach me how to make progress spiritually.

A profession, but not a calling

I remember sitting around with my mother trying to figure out what I should be—or rather, what I should do. I told her I wanted to help people. But I didn't love school and didn't want to be a doctor. I was active, so couldn't imagine myself sitting at a desk. Then Mom read about physical therapy. It seemed like a good idea, but it was a practical decision rather than a passion. Through all the years as a PT, my search for work that was my calling continued beneath the surface. It wasn't until I began to invite elders into my home that I found my real vocation.

It was during my early work as a physical therapist that I began to be interested in the patients I worked with as more than just their functionality. As a PT, my primary job was to help the patient be as safely mobile as possible, to help them learn to use their limbs again after an accident or a stroke. I became increasingly aware of the importance of taking time to do the little extras that make a difference: I'd pick up the tissues that had inadvertently fallen to the floor, put an address book where it could be easily reached, or get an extra sweater for warmth.

As I began to take care of these little outer disturbances that trouble us all—and which their conditions prevented them from taking care of for themselves—it became more and more apparent that the resulting peace of mind, coupled with the inner desire to mobilize, promoted the emergence of a person's renewed ability to walk safely. And with this came the growing desire to work with the whole person.

My second job, at Glendale Adventist Medical Center, involved seeing people for up to six weeks at a time in Rehabilitation, frequently after they had had strokes. Sometimes their speech was slurred. They couldn't say what they wanted to. But, over time, I got to know them and saw that, despite their disability, the essence of the person was still there. It was then I started to explore the issue of wholeness and identity: Who are you, I wondered, if you've had a stroke or an amputation? Does the essence of a person change with such physical or mental damage?

A speech therapist, Leslie Madrona, and I came up with the idea of having a day program in which we would have a chance to work with the whole person. We met a couple of times, realized it wasn't practical for us to do, and abandoned the idea. But it was then that the seed was planted.

The seed was in hibernation for a long time. I left Southern California and moved to Seattle in the mid-80s. I worked at the Veteran's Hospital, got married, had a baby. I worked at a home care agency and then a continuing care community in Seattle doing physical therapy with the residents. I had two more children. Then three things came together: My husband remodeled the kitchen, and suddenly we had a more open, functional space. My youngest child started kindergarten. And I was ready to decrease my hours as a physical therapist. Plus I had a few more tools in my toolkit than when I was in my early twenties: I had a spiritual practice from Vedanta. I had read some of the materials grounded in Anthroposophy from the Waldorf School—particularly one small book I've referred to often in these pages, *The Fulfillment of Old Age* by Norbert Glas—and had experienced the Waldorf School philosophy through my children's time there. I also began to be interested in the conscious aging movement and what Rabbi Zalman Schachter-Shalomi called Spiritual Eldering. These experiences, plus my many years of work as a therapist, culminated with an idea: I will start something here, in our home.

My home with my husband had always been open to others, a place where neighborhood kids came in and out, people borrowed and shared. We knew our neighbors. Kids did their homework at the central table in the house— what became the Elderwise table. So when I felt called to starting a day program for frail elders, it didn't actually seem like that big of a deal to invite elders into our home. Many families open their homes to children, taking in extra kids. This was a similar concept: take in some neighborhood elders and create a stimulating, warm, creative, enriching environment and opportunities for growth.

Shortly after the idea came, I was at a Vedanta retreat property in Arlington, Washington, a fairly rustic place in those days. I saw an older woman struggling up an uneven hillside at the top of which were the rest rooms. She was not someone I knew, but, without hesitating or even thinking about it, I went to her side and supported her up the hill. At the top, I turned around. My guru was watching us with a soft smile on his wise face. That smile felt like a blessing, and I understood that the blessing was for more than that one act: it was a blessing on my vision of working with older adults.

Making my vision a reality

Carrying that blessing with me, we went to work. I invited my friend Cally Fulton, whose daughter was in my daughter's class at the Waldorf School, to join me in this endeavor: founding Elderwise. Her partnership at this stage was invaluable. In addition to remodeling the kitchen, a wheelchair path and a little ramp were installed leading to the back door for those who couldn't walk up the four steps to the front door. We put rails in our living room for standing exercises. At first, we thought that the coffee and teatime was a precursor to the actual program, an opportunity to get settled and ready. But we soon came to see that it was, in fact, an essential part of the program.

My parents were downsizing and getting rid of the silver teapots they had received as wedding presents. They pulled them out of the things they were selling and gave them to me. We bought dishes with an ivy pattern, of which

I still have a few precious plates and bowls. The teacups are all gone. We used all that for about twelve years. We cooked, usually one-pot meals: soup and salad, chili. In those early days, I would get up early, clean the house, get the kids off to school somehow, and make a pot of soup for the Elderwise lunch.

We started with a real *Can do!* attitude. I asked a neighbor if she would pose for a flyer. She said fine—as long as she didn't have to go to any meetings!—so our first flyer is my neighbor holding a paintbrush. We posted those flyers in apartment buildings; we leafleted neighborhoods. It was a little bit unorthodox. In some ways it was actually quite revolutionary, even though it was also quite ordinary: we were just inviting neighbors into a home.

A handful of people responded to our flyers: Don and Nancy and Alex, Stina and Willit, Marie and Ann. The beginning of a group.

At first we met one day a week, without a particular focus on dementia (though I must have had some thought about it, because I did consult with some people at the Alzheimer's Association), then added a second day. As we created an environment and activities enriching for older adults, we were conscious of deliberately looking at the whole person and developing a new model. We focused on growth and development. We did art at the dining room table. We either stayed there for discussions or visits from guests with expertise in various fields—farmers, gardeners, cooks, musicians, dancers— or moved the group to the guest room.

Sometimes we just had two or three people and would sit around the table in the kitchen and have tea. One day, someone was hungry. All I had in the house was a stale bagel. So I toasted it, spread it with peanut butter and jam… and it became a tradition. Since then, every day at Elderwise we share toast and peanut butter. It wasn't the stale bagel that was so good: it was sharing it in community.

The group expanded and revealed itself as individuals. Marie had a great spaghetti recipe and was always cautioning everyone, "You be careful now." Betty was a ceramist who made beautiful works of art. Alex was super-considerate and thoughtful. Don did the best he could with his poor vision. We had another wonderful artist in Nancy. Stina got lost in her artwork. Willet was an amazing person, and Ann's attitude was, "If you can't do it right, don't do it."

We certainly weren't doing it for the money. When Cally had to step away, I was fortunate to find others to work with me. Inside, it felt like I was meant to do this, more than any "work" I had done before. This was not "something to do"—this was what I was *supposed to do*. I knew it was a crazy idea, that it wasn't practical and didn't make any "sense." But I kept going. I never questioned it: it was meant to happen. Now, over two decades later, I am grateful that, despite the challenges, I had the opportunity to learn and grow, as I shared this path with so many participants and colleagues. We have all been enriched by our journey together.

APPENDIX 2:

Reflections on facilitating art
The Elderwise Way

by Fran Dunlap, founding Elderwise facilitator and artist

Once you have the materials, it is the attitude of the facilitator that is most important. The experience will be mutually rewarding if you, too, fully participate in the creative journey. I look at each art session as an experiment, a chance for us to discover something together. I have to be excited and engaged before I can expect the participants to be engaged in the work of art. It's the honorable approach: If I don't take it seriously, why should you?

One can prepare by becoming more aware of nature: the color, the light, the seasons. Then work to bring this excitement, this feeling, this *aha moment,* alive in the art room.

That awareness of nature is as rewarding for some individuals as the *how do I paint a tree*—the intellectual or cognitive—approach to creating artwork. Persons living with memory loss often find great satisfaction in the feeling realm. They can live from within the color.

Using a limited palette of blue, red, and yellow (with occasional additions) expands the flexibility of experience and imagination. Through mixing, there are endless varieties of greens, oranges, and purples. This gives the painter both surprises and the opportunity to make, and remake, choices.

The wet paper frees us from the fear of "having to draw something." We can always blame it on the water. Or, in a happier case, the water is our friend; colors flow into new shapes, and the imagination sparkles.

I usually come prepared with an idea of what we will paint, although on occasion I change gears completely when someone comes in with an inspiring story or interesting show-and-tell. In that situation, you start with one person who is completely engaged, and then that person's enthusiasm can help bring the others along. Flexibility is important.

After deciding what art project I want to experience with the group, I consider how to start: *What color will I use to begin?* always conscious of how colors overlay to produce still other colors. The tree shape could initially start with a blue; as the sun (yellow) hits it, suddenly it's green.

The mountains can be red, depending on their make-up and the time of day—for example, sunrise or sunset—and then become purple with the addition of blue.

There is nothing we can paint, odd as it may look to us, that hasn't occurred somewhere in nature.

I like to choose subjects for painting that correspond with the season or with local themes. With participants coming from all over the world, there may be many different perspectives on the given subject.

There was Sara from Alaska, who happily painted a yellow river and picket-like pine trees, while I, absorbed in my own art, envisioned the blue river and tall pines from my Maine experience. I encouraged Sara to make the pines taller and asked her, *Why is the river yellow?* When I went to Alaska several years later, I said, *Sara was right!*

It's important to me that the painters feel pleased with their results. If someone seems stuck or puzzled, I sometimes offer guidance in the form of a suggestion about color or design. It may free the painter to go on in a positive, hopeful frame of mind. At other times, someone might follow my suggestion and then feel that it wrecked what they were aiming for. No one gets it right every time!

In my experience, preselected ideas about subjects often result in the most beautiful and satisfying paintings, even when that initial concept is just used to get the creative juices flowing.

I try to alternate *scenes* and *still life*. Scenes that have a path leading back into a field or mountains allow the painter to "go there." The still life subjects work best if they engage us emotionally on some level—say, through puzzlement or surprise—as when we put on the table an unexpected shoe, a fish bowl with a fish swimming around in it, eggs, or steam rising from a mug.

I've noticed that most of the people I work with stop looking outward at the object when they start to paint. It's as if they have digested the image and now look inward for confirmation.

The paintings are important, but so is the artists' pride in their finished artwork and the feeling of success conveyed in describing what they intended. The time we take at the end of the art session, or at the beginning of the next, to admire each other's paintings is as important to the process as the act of creation itself.

BIBLIOGRAPHY

Aronson, Louise. *Elderhood: Redefining Aging, Transforming Medicine, Reimagining Life.* Bloomsbury Publishing. 2019.

Arrien, Angeles. *The Second Half of Life: Opening the Eight Gates of Wisdom.* Sounds True. 2007.

Bateson, Mary Catherine. *Composing a Further Life: The Age of Active Wisdom.* Vintage. 2011.

Camps, Annegret; Hagenhoff, Brigitte; van der Star, Ada. *Anthroposophical Care for the Elderly.* Floris Books. 2009.

Chittister, Joan. *The Gift of Years: Growing Older Gracefully.* BlueBridge. 2010.

Cohen, Gene D., M.D. *The Creative Age: Awakening Human Potential in the Second Half of Life.* William Morrow & Company. 2000.

Fischer, Kathleen. *Winter Grace: Spirituality of Aging.* Upper Room Books. 1998.

Glas, Norbert, M.D. *The Fulfillment of Old Age.* Anthroposophic Press; 1970.

Helfgott, Esther Altshul, PhD. *Dear Alzheimer's: A Caregiver's Diary & Poems.* Cave Moon Press. 2013.

Leder, Drew. *Spiritual Passages: Embracing Life's Sacred Journey.* Putnam. 1997.

Lustbader, Wendy. *Counting on Kindness: The Dilemmas of Dependency.* NY Free Press. 1991.

McLeod, Beth Witrogen. *Caregiving: The Spiritual Journey of Love, Loss, and Renewal.* John Wiley and Sons. 1999.

Remen, Rachel Naomi. *My Grandfather's Blessings: Stories of Strength, Refuge and Belonging.* Riverhead Books. 2001.

Remen, Rachel Naomi. *Kitchen Table Wisdom: Stories That Heal.* Riverhead Books. 2006.

Richards, Marty. *Caresharing: A Reciprocal Approach to Caregiving and Care Receiving in the Complexities of Aging, Illness or Disability.* Skylight Paths Publishing. 2011.

Richmond, Lewis. *Aging As A Spiritual Practice: A Contemplative Guide to Growing Older and Wiser.* Gotham Books. 2012.

Rupp, Joyce. *Praying Our Goodbyes: Understanding the Spirituality of Change in Our Lives.* Ivy Books. 1988.

Sadler, B., and Ridenour, A. *Transforming the Healthcare Experience Through the Arts.* Aesthetics. 2008.

Schacter-Shalomi, Zalman, and Miller, Ronald S. *From Age-ing to Sage-ing: A Revolutionary Approach to Growing Older.* Grand Central Publishing. 2014.

Snowdon, David. *Aging with Grace: What the Nun Study Teaches Us About Leading Longer, Healthier, and More Meaningful Lives.* Bantam Books. 2001.

Soesman, Albert. *Our Twelve Senses: How Healthy Senses Refresh the Soul.* Hawthorn Press. 1998.

Srode, Molly. *Creating a Spiritual Retirement: A Guide to the Unseen Possibilities in Our Lives.* Skylight Paths Publishing. 2003.

Steiner, Rudolf. *Growing Old: The Spiritual Dimensions of Aging.* Rudolf Steiner Press. 2019.

Thibault, Jane Marie. *A Deepening Love Affair: The Gift of God in Later Life.* Upper Room Books. 1993.

Thomas, William H., Jr. *What are Old People For? How Elders Will Save the World.* Vanderwyck & Burnham. 2007

Tornstam, Lars. *Gerotranscendence: A Developmental Theory of Positive Aging.* Spring Publishing, Inc. 2005.